SUPER
SEARCHER
AUTHOR
SCRIBE

SUPER
SEARCHER
AUTHOR
SCRIBE

Successful Writers Share Their
INTERNET RESEARCH SECRETS

Loraine Page
Edited by Reva Basch

CyberAge Books

Information Today, Inc.
Medford, New Jersey

First Printing, 2002

Super Searcher, Author, Scribe:
Successful Writers Share Their Internet Research Secrets

Copyright © 2002 by Loraine Page

Super Searchers, Volume IX
A series edited by Reva Basch

A CIP catalog record for this book is available from the Library of Congress.

Printed and bound in the United States of America

Publisher: Thomas H. Hogan, Sr.
Editor-in-Chief: John B. Bryans
Managing Editor: Deborah Poulson
Copy Editor: Dorothy Pike
Production Manager: M. Heide Dengler
Cover Designer: Jacqueline Walter
Book Designer: Kara Mia Jalkowski
Indexer: Lori Lathrop

Dedication

To Ed for being there for me from the beginning—
the date we met and the date of this book contract are the same.
I hope you'll be with me always.

About *The Super Searchers Web Page*

At the Information Today Web site, you will find *The Super Searchers Web Page*, featuring links to sites mentioned in this book. We will periodically update the page, removing dead links and adding additional sites that may be useful to readers.

The Super Searchers Web Page is being made available as a bonus to readers of *Super Searcher, Author, Scribe* and other books in the Super Searchers series. To access the page, an Internet connection and Web browser are required. Go to:

www.infotoday.com/supersearchers

Table of Contents

Foreword

Anyone who has visited my office can attest that I am an expert on search. I'd have to be; how else could I find anything buried in those stacks of papers, those arrays of strewn file folders, that grand memo and manuscript organizer I call my floor?

I look up from that floor at the Internet browser on my computer screen and see figuratively the same thing—a jumbled morass of facts and information and comments and notes. The Web seems unfathomable and unorganizable, just like my paper system. It isn't called the World Wide Filing Cabinet, after all.

But, just as with my paper filing system, "haphazardly organized" and "unfindable" are *not* synonymous. You just gotta know where to look.

More importantly, you must know *how* to look.

That's why I enjoyed reading *Super Searcher, Author, Scribe*. There's no one *how* in searching the Internet (nor my piles of papers, for that matter). Different approaches, different ways of thinking, different source portals all come into play, and the writers interviewed herein exemplify the many differences and demonstrate different search strategies and philosophies. Look over their shoulders as they conduct their work—it's a great way to learn.

My primary search tip lies in extending my observation about knowing where and *how* to look. For the writer, the most important element of search is knowing *what to do with what you find*. Ask yourself these questions:

Do you trust what you find on the Web? A recent poll indicated that the U.S. public places less trust in information from the Internet than they do in information from magazines, newspapers, and television. I agree with placing less trust in Internet information—nonprofessional "editors" put far more unfiltered and unquestioned info out onto the Web than we'd like to believe possible. I'm not implying that all info out there is unreliable (the work of professional editors proliferates on the Web, too), but as is good journalistic practice in general, don't just find it—confirm it.

Does your manuscript need what you find on the Web? And more importantly, does your reader need it? Many writers feel pressure to include all the information they find during their research. "It was a lot of work finding this stuff! I can't let it go to waste!" Yet, it's a bigger waste when irrelevant or redundant research finds its way into print. I believe it was Frank Lloyd Wright who said, "You have got to stop thinking that just because you worked very hard on something, that is reason enough to think it has some worth." (Did he really say that? Hey, I found it on the Web—it must be true!)

So, you as a writer are faced in this medium with the same challenges you face with all others. Get the facts, get the facts right, and communicate the important facts to your reader. Solid Internet search strategies will help you in the first two steps. The third step is up to you.

(And when you finally find what you need, do what I do. Print out a copy, throw it on a pile somewhere over near the ficus tree, and pray you can find it later.)

William Brohaugh
New Media Director, F&W Publications, WritersDigest.com
Former editor of *Writer's Digest* magazine and Writer's Digest Books

Acknowledgments

Minutes count when you're on deadline, and most of the authors I interviewed for this book were on deadline when I contacted them. I will always be grateful to them for their generosity in sparing some of those minutes for this project. I know they didn't like many of my questions—they looked too much like essay questions from school! I think they overcame their initial hesitancy when they realized that their answers could help other writers. That's what writers do—they share what they know for the benefit of others.

Thanks go to John Bryans, who said yes immediately after I presented the idea for this book to him. He welcomed the concept of including authors into the realm of super searchers.

Reva Basch is the best editor anyone could have. Her equanimity, sense of humor, and impeccable editing skills make her a national treasure. A gifted writer and researcher herself, she guided this book to completion with a sure hand.

I want to thank Gary Stern, a friend and full-time freelance writer, for his encouraging emails throughout the writing of this book, and for his suggestions of writers to contact.

I also want to thank Sheryl Heller and Mike Avery of Twin Peaks Geeks for keeping my Macintosh in top shape for writing.

And finally, thank you, Monica, for being the best daughter ever. You've always believed in me and you've always been there for me.

Introduction

What are writers doing with regard to the Internet? That's the simple question this book addresses as it provides a platform for fourteen diverse authors to talk about how they utilize computer technology and online resources for their own research purposes.

Only one writer in this book is also a professional searcher with a library science degree. The others are self-taught—like me and, quite probably, you—with varying degrees of skill. In this regard, *Super Searcher, Author, Scribe* is different from the other books in the "Super Searcher" series published by CyberAge Books and edited by veteran searcher/author Reva Basch. Those books contain Q&A interviews with professional searchers in such fields as medicine, law, business, broadcasting, and stock trading.

On these pages, you'll meet writers whose computer skills will knock your socks off; they're referred to by others, and sometimes by themselves, as computer nerds. One was called an Internet phenom by a fellow writer. Others you'll meet might remind you more of yourself, if you're a beginner. One says she's a baby user, and another referred to himself as a technopeasant.

You'll hear what these working writers have to say about our new technology and how it has changed their lives. They love the Internet and consider it an incredible timesaver, but they haven't abandoned the old-fashioned methods of researching—yet. They can see that a sea change is approaching—one in which digital technology will replace, in many instances, their beloved print pages—and, for the most part, they are facing it calmly, bravely, and with optimism.

I am grateful to the writers for the time they devoted to answering my questions. I used email to contact most of them initially and, yes, even interviewed most of them that way. Hey, they're writers! Let them do what they do best. I admit I'm an inveterate email user. I felt vindicated when author David Weinberger, questioned as to what part email plays in his career, replied, "Most of what I know I learned through email."

Most of the authors balked when I asked them to recreate their searches, claiming it was too hard to recount an action that occurs at lightning speed. With some nudging, they divulged the particulars, including the URLs for Web sites they mentioned. It's always good to hear about other people's favorite Web sites; it helps us to cull from the overwhelming number of sites out there. *Newsday,* my daily newspaper on Long Island, is aware of the benefits of this type of sharing. Each week the paper publishes "My Bookmarks," a column that lists the favorite Web sites of interesting people like playwrights, artists, singers, chefs, and other local celebrities.

Interviewing a hodgepodge of people who write for a living and who are not professional researchers has resulted in a book where the topics under discussion range from the how-tos of straightforward factual research projects to more exotic tasks like viewing prison inmates' photographs or igniting spirited email discussion with a provocative statement on your Web site for the purpose of publishing it in your zine. It's hard to draw generalizations because each author uses the Internet in whichever way works for his or her personality and way of writing. Nevertheless, I'll attempt to draw some general conclusions and observations about the most important of the many topics we discussed.

Usefulness of the Internet

As I said, each author uses the Internet for his or her unique purposes. But most of them go online to grab a quick fact and to obtain leads. Even the most ardent library lovers admit that nothing beats the Internet for its accessibility, number of sources in one place, and speed. In other words, you walk into a room in your own house, type in a word, and—boom—you may have your answer in under a minute!

The writers—mind you, these are writers who are getting published regularly, so they are good—are unanimous in feeling that they can't use the

Internet for the "flavor" or "color" that they like to infuse into their work. They say the Internet is useful because it can connect them with leads—people who will be valuable to them if they can follow up with a phone call or an in-person interview. It's this closer interaction that gives their writing a feel of authenticity. Novelist Jodi Picoult says she cultivated a source she found in an online discussion forum to the point where she was finally invited to an Amish dairy farm to milk cows in the wee hours of the morning. It was of enormous help in the writing of *Plain Truth*.

Search Engines

Hands down, Google is the winner. Who wouldn't like a search engine that delivers just about all the time? That said, some of the writers are still using whatever search engine they started with a few years ago. Others, more sophisticated in their computer use, turn to different search engines for different purposes. Alfred Glossbrenner, who has written personal computer books since the early days of the technology, says you have to pick the best tool for the job. His advice: "It pays to read the online help and search tips provided at the search site." That's true, and ideally we should all strive to do that. But some of the writers say they can't be bothered reading documentation. They just plunge right in and learn as they go.

When I asked for search tips, the answer I got most often was that, assuming you are using an appropriate search engine, you have to learn how to phrase your search query so that the most relevant hits pop to the top of your results list. Who wants to face a list of literally thousands of items and have to paw through them all for the good stuff? It's not only a daunting prospect that might make you want to run for the hills instead of complete your writing project, but it's a waste of your valuable time.

Accuracy

I asked the authors how comfortable they felt using the information they found on the Internet. I found they all wanted reliable information, but it was the nonfiction writers, naturally, rather than the novelists and poets, who felt that accuracy was absolutely crucial in their line of work.

The way the writers approach the accuracy concern is to be wary of personal Web sites—fan sites, that sort of thing—and to be more trusting of information coming from an established organization's Web site. They also agree that you can trust a fact if you visit two or three other trustworthy sites and find the same answer.

Reference Resources

Some of the writers still like the kind of reference resources that are heavy to lift and sit somewhere in the vicinity of their desks. They don't mind thumbing through those well-worn pages; it's simply what they're used to. Bonnie Remsberg, nonfiction writer and playwright, swears by her copy of *Webster's New World Word Book*, which includes spellings of about 30,000 most-used words.

Others are venturesome and have figured out where to go online for word definitions, synonyms, foreign words, and the like. Nonfiction writer and editor David Fryxell found an online reference resource that provides clichés, listed by subject matter. The much-maligned cliché, he says, actually can be useful when trying to craft a witty headline.

All of the writers say they use the dictionary installed in their word processor some or all of the time. And many turn to the Encyclopaedia Britannica Web site for fact checking, but not for in-depth research.

Finding Articles Online

Again, some of the writers like to find newspaper and magazine articles the old-fashioned way—by visiting a bricks-and-mortar library. Others enjoy logging onto the Web sites of the country's major newspapers. Here they can find the full text of current articles for free, and archived ones for a fee.

Some of the writers don't mind paying a fee to a commercial service like LexisNexis, Dialog, or Dow Jones. Detective/crime writer Ridley Pearson turned to LexisNexis for information on illegal organ harvesting and received fifty articles from around the world dealing with probable cases of that particular crime. It was enough for him to get started on his novel *The Angel Maker*.

But cost is a factor for these writers, and if they can get the facts or the articles somewhere for free, naturally that's what they'll do. Paula Berinstein, who writes books and articles while working as a professional researcher, implied that if money were of no concern, then Dialog would be number one. Says Paula, "Dialog has about the best content you'll find anywhere. The array of databases is staggering."

Communication

Email: Where would these writers be without it? That's the feeling I got from the interviews. Online communication is invaluable to them. It's a timesaver; jot a quick note, get a quick note back. It's an expander; it opens up contacts to a universe of people they might not otherwise have met. It's a social avenue; writing is a lonely profession and emailing fills a need they have for contact with other people, even if it's just silliness and banter about nonessential topics.

A few of the writers expressed concern that we may be getting so tuned into the digital word that we forget to go out and meet people face to face. But all of them agree that the benefits of email outweigh that type of concern. "Writing a book without email would take years longer. It's so hard to get in touch with people otherwise," says Paula Berinstein.

Gary Gach, a poet and nonfiction writer who is working on a book about China, says that email is indispensable for his career. He says, "I've emailed chapters and sections to experts for a critique, which has often come back in another color or as ongoing email dialogue. Email is terrific for collaborative work in a short period of time across various time zones."

Discussion groups: Gary also says that online discussion groups, in which members post questions and answers, are also valuable to him. He enthuses about one that focuses on Buddhism, a core interest: "The Buddhist Peace Fellowship has a sweet combination of news, events notices, and occasional impromptu discussion for folks around the world. … As with all lists, a main topic (thread) can be the jumping-off point for various and sundry human affairs, branching off, looping the loop, and fanning out in all sorts of interesting byways."

Chat: The online discussion group or mailing list is not to be confused with "chat," which is real time. Jodi Picoult says she sometimes enters a chat room to talk with her fans. She likes it, she says, because she can do it in her pajamas and have lots of fun while getting important feedback about her books.

Personal Web Sites

Nonfiction writer and Internet searcher extraordinaire Sarah Wernick says that having your own Web site is like "having a business card with a portfolio of writing samples attached."

Some of the very computer-savvy writers you'll find in this book advocate learning how to write, design, and post your own Web site. They say they really enjoyed the process. Do not fear; you don't have to do it yourself if you don't want to! You can hire people to do it for you.

The major benefit of having your own Web site if you are a writer is that you can publicize your work. You can also make yourself accessible to fans and contacts in the publishing world by providing an email address on the site for people who want to write to you.

Technophobia

Many of the writers I talked to admit knowing other writers who are apprehensive about using the Internet. They are surprised by this and feel that a writer who is not making use of the Internet is missing out on a whole new world—a world they'd actually be thrilled with if they only gave it a chance. Author David Weinberger of *Cluetrain Manifesto* fame is succinct on this subject: "If you're writing something that occasionally touches upon the factual world, you can learn more, faster, on the Web than in the real world."

Reid Goldsborough, who writes a syndicated column about computers and certainly qualifies as an Internet expert, confesses: "If I speak glibly about this, it's because I once was technophobic myself. … Over time, I experienced one 'Eureka!' moment after another as I discovered how my PC could help me do what I wanted to do."

Only a Tool

This last comment by Reid Goldsborough sums up what the writers are saying about the Internet—it's only a tool. They'd much rather be writing than talking about a tool, however interesting that tool may be. Carpenters don't want to talk about a hammer, after all. They'd rather talk about what they're building. As Reid sums up in a pithy quote: "I'm a writer first, nerd second."

I can't blame the writers for finding my questions difficult. I'm relieved that no one asked me how *I* do online searching. I'm not an expert. I'm only a little older than a "baby user," even though I've been using a computer since 1980. Just this morning when I sat down to write this, I dragged my Eudora email application to the trash icon by mistake—and then emptied the trash. I'm the longtime editor of *Link-Up* [146, see Appendix], a bimonthly print magazine that's been covering online services since the early days, and I am bombarded with press releases every day. All that information on the latest developments in computers and online technology hasn't translated into a natural ability at searching.

But I do go online—constantly. Practice makes perfect, I hope. I search on the Internet for my work as a freelance editor and writer, and I search on the Internet for anything that pops up in my personal life. I'm hooked. And so are the writers who share their online experiences here. Watching over their shoulders as they carry out the very important business of research, the foundation of writing, can only benefit us.

If you're a writer, you're probably a reader. And if you don't get anything else out of this book, at least you will be introduced, as I was, to writers in genres you might not read on a regular basis. They cover the gamut—detective fiction, historical romance, popular fiction, poetry, sociology, writing instruction, computers, and science.

If you're a writer, you're undoubtedly also curious to see what other writers are accomplishing and how they've gotten to where they are today. If this is the case, you'll love reading their bios, which in most cases are in their own words.

Again, I want to thank the writers for taking time out of their hectic lives to get involved with this project. They are here, in these pages, in part because they are accessible to their readers. They have Web sites or email addresses or both, thus choosing to make themselves available to the public. Some writers, I found when beginning the research for this book, prefer to stay hidden from their fans, and tell their publicists to say no to interviews.

The writers I interviewed are not afraid to try new technology. In my search for potential interviewees, I found some authors who aren't even using a computer yet. One, Elmore Leonard—who has written more best-selling mysteries than I can count—was kind enough to refer me to his researcher, whom you'll meet in Chapter Four.

The writers in this book agreed to talk about how they do research. They didn't promise anything more. In fact, when they learned the title of the book and that it was to be one in a series of books about "super searchers," many hesitated. They claimed they couldn't live up to the title. But if you listen carefully, you'll come away with secrets they didn't know they possessed.

Sarah Wernick

Medical Writer and Internet Devotee

Sarah Wernick is a freelance writer with a Ph.D. in sociology and a repetitive strain injury in her right hand from spending way too much time online. In a previous life, Sarah taught sociology at, among other places, Washington University and Northeastern University. She abandoned academia in 1978 to write professionally, starting with articles in a local tabloid throwaway and eventually graduating to *Woman's Day*, *Working Mother*, *Smithsonian*, the *New York Times*, and other national publications. She's served as contributing editor at *Working Mother* and *Chocolate News*. Among her article awards is the 1997 American Medical Association President's Prize for excellence in tobacco reporting for "The Silent Killer," published in *Ladies' Home Journal*. This was the first feature article about lung cancer to appear in a major women's magazine.

These days, Sarah focuses on writing books. She's currently finishing *Lung Cancer: Myths, Facts, Choices—and Hope* for Norton, co-authored with Claudia Henschke, M.D., of Cornell University and Peggy McCarthy, founder of the Alliance for Lung Cancer Advocacy, Support, and Education. Previous projects include three bestsellers about strength training for mature women, all written with Miriam Nelson of Tufts University: *Strong Women Stay Young* (Bantam, 1997 and 2000), *Strong Women Stay Slim* (Bantam, 1998), and *Strong Women, Strong Bones* (Putnam, 2000), which was a Books for a Better Life award winner in 2000. Sarah's other co-authored book, *The Emotional Problems of Normal Children* (Bantam, 1994), a collaboration with Stanley Turecki, M.D., was honored by *Child* magazine as one of the best parenting books of 1994.

Sarah is a member of the American Society of Journalists and Authors, the Authors Guild, and the National Writers Union. She's based in the Boston area of Massachusetts and can be enticed to leave her computer by chocolate or opportunities to speak on book proposals, collaborative writing, and Internet research.

sarah@sarahwernick.com
www.sarahwernick.com

What part has online research played in your writing, both books and articles?

I use the Internet constantly, not only for research but also for connecting with colleagues, reaching people to interview, marketing my work, shopping, not to mention goofing off. At this point, I no longer remember how I worked before I was online. When a nonfiction writer tells me, "Oh yeah, the Internet is pretty good, but I don't find it all that useful," I figure this person hasn't yet discovered what's out there.

There's never been a resource like this in the history of the world. Every major institution—governments, businesses, universities, libraries, museums, organizations, newspapers, magazines, TV, and radio stations—has an online presence, often with extensive information. On top of that, hundreds of thousands of individuals share their expertise with extraordinary generosity. The best library in the world can't compare, not only because the Internet is so much larger, but also because it's so readily searched. And everything is instantly available, right at your desk, any time of day or night.

How did you get started?

In 1983 I bought a Kaypro computer. The operating system came with twenty-five mimeographed pages of unintelligible nerd-speak. In desperation, I joined the Boston Computer Society's Kaypro User Group, which had a terrific online forum. When we ran into trouble, we could crank up our modems, dial in, and get advice. I still remember one frantic message from an unfortunate journalist on deadline: "Help!!! I just ran the spellcheck program, and it turned my article into an alphabetized list of words."

In the early 1990s, I joined CompuServe and started using its resources for article research. For example, I was asked to write an article for *Woman's Day* about mothers who were secretly disappointed in their child. Normally I'd interview friends or mothers I met at my children's school. But how could I walk up to a woman and ask, "Hey, are you bummed out because your kid is a loser?" I left a tactfully worded message on a CompuServe parenting forum and several members offered to speak with me.

During this period, I was writing a monthly health news column for *Working Mother* magazine. Practically all my leads came from CompuServe's Executive News Service, which screens major wire services and press releases for stories containing any keywords you specify.

These days I use the Internet rather than CompuServe; they've dropped most of their research services and their forums have shrunk. However, Executive News Service is still very valuable for keeping up with news of interest. I often get word on new studies before my expert co-authors spot them in medical journals.

Where did you turn for information about lung cancer?

The best starting point for online research on lung cancer is a remarkable Web site called Lung Cancer Online [151, see Appendix], set up by a patient. Karen Parles, who's a professional research librarian, was diagnosed three years ago at age thirty-eight. She provides a terrific collection of links to authoritative information, beautifully organized and clearly annotated. Doctors use it too.

For background information, I've tapped general medical resources like Medscape [162], which provides access to Medline's vast store of medical citations and abstracts, and the *Merck Manual Home Edition*, the full text of which is online [163]. I've also relied on cancer-specific sources, such as the National Cancer Institute [170], Oncolink from the University of Pennsylvania [188], the American Cancer Society [19], the Association for Cancer Online Resources [29], which has superb patient discussion groups, and CancerBACUP [49] in the U.K., which I probably never would have seen without the Internet.

They have wonderful resources, such as a compassionate book-let for parents with cancer called *What Do I Tell the Children?*

Steve Dunn's Cancer Guide [238] is another outstanding patient site. Steve was diagnosed with advanced kidney cancer in 1989. He saved his life by researching his disease and finding a new treatment, which was then in clinical trials. He offers excellent how-to advice about online medical research plus savvy suggestions for people interested in joining clinical trials.

Can you really rely on medical information from patients? That seems risky.

Good patient sites carefully avoid giving specific medical advice. They link to reliable resources; they urge readers to talk with their doctor. Patients are often the best source for nitty-gritty practical suggestions. If I want tips on coping with hair loss during chemotherapy, I'm not going to find them in the *New England Journal of Medicine.*

Much of what's available online comes from the same trust-worthy sources I'd use at the Harvard Medical School Library. Of course, there's also a lot of crap out there. You have to consider the source and use common sense. But that's true of medical information in any medium. I'm annoyed by dire warnings—usually from people who haven't a clue about all the great stuff online—implying that the Internet is uniquely unreliable. Apparently these folks have never watched an infomercial or read the claims on supplement labels in a health food store.

When I was researching the lung cancer book, I came across sites with testimonials for various "cures," such as an herbal brew whose recipe was given to a Canadian nurse by an ancient Indian medicine man. In the book, we suggest that readers talk to their doctor about claims like this or check them out on Quack Watch [209], a health-related anti-scam site.

What's your favorite search engine—the one you go to instinctively?

I don't go to one search engine instinctively; I go to the one that seems best suited to the particular search I'm doing. This is something I've learned—and that I'm still learning—by lots of practice.

The search engine I use most is Google [104]. Another good one is FAST [93], but I have a Google toolbar, available free from their Web site, installed in my browser, so I'm always ready to run a Google search. Google is best for finding the leading sites on a particular topic. The pages they list first are the ones that other sites link to most often. So, in effect, all the people who create Web site links are helping to determine Google's rankings. Another advantage of Google is that it caches, or stores, Web pages. This lets me see expired pages, which normally aren't available.

But Google isn't best for everything. For example, when I needed to find a hotel in Lenox, Massachusetts, I used Yahoo! [277], because Yahoo! indexes pages by topic, so it gave me a tidy list of links to hotels in Lenox. If I were trying to find an article about Al Gore that was written after the election, I'd use HotBot [115], which lets me specify date limits like "in the last 6 months." Otherwise I'd be swamped with irrelevant pre-election hits.

Northern Light [185] and Vivisimo [262] subdivide hits by subtopics. That's very useful for search terms that have multiple meanings. For example, one of the patients I interviewed for the lung cancer book told me about a play called *Wit*, and I wanted to learn more about it. I used Northern Light for that search, because I figured it would be easier to focus on relevant hits. Sure enough, the search results included a "Theater and per-forming arts" category. When I clicked on that, I found the play immediately.

If I strike out with Google, I try one of the metasearch engines, like Dogpile [76] or Ask Jeeves [27]. These give results from mul-tiple search engines, so they often return too many irrelevant hits. But they're perfect when I want broad coverage. A couple of years ago I wanted to send a funny cheering-up gift to a col-league who'd been through a bad experience. I had seen a T-shirt decorated with pictures of bird droppings, which seemed exactly right. So I surfed over to Ask Jeeves, which lets you type in your question in plain English, and wrote: "Where can I buy a bird shit T-shirt?" In less than a minute I'd found the Web site of a nature store on Cape Cod that carried the shirt.

No search engine covers everything that's online. With obscure topics, a specialized search engine might be best. There's an extraordinary list of specialty search engines at Leiden University [142]. A less complete but also less overwhelming option is Search IQ [230]. When I see these lists, I realize how much I still don't know. But I try to keep up with new developments by occasionally checking the Search Engine Watch Web site [229]. Mostly, though, I've learned by experimenting and paying attention to what works best.

Do you use online reference sources like dictionaries, encyclopedias, thesauri, or quotation finders?

Yes, but only occasionally. I have Microsoft Bookshelf on CD-ROM, whose dictionary and thesaurus I consult often. For the lung cancer book, I sometimes used the online version of Encarta [84] or the Encyclopaedia Britannica [85] for basic scientific background.

I find online reference sources particularly handy when I need a tidbit from a reference work I'd never buy, such as a dictionary of symbols [242] or a dictionary of Australian slang [31]. I've learned about available reference materials from two sites in particular: Reference Desk [217] provides extensive links to reference materials available online, and Your Dictionary [281] has a large collection of links to online dictionaries of all kinds, including many medical dictionaries.

Speaking of dictionaries, I can't resist mentioning the amazing list of hundreds of ways to say "vomit" (e.g., "talking to Ralph on the big white telephone") I found at LaughNet [141].

Back to more serious business, now that telephone directory assistance is so expensive—and unreliable—I always check phone numbers online. Online directories also provide addresses and more flexibility about searching. For example, if I have a phone number, I can search a reverse directory for the name and address. The directory I use most is AnyWho [23].

Online discussion groups sometimes develop excellent FAQs—answers to Frequently Asked Questions. I was once asked to put together a proposal about roller coasters. I found everything I needed from an FAQ [224]. Of course, the groups are also a way to find people to interview. A good discussion group resource is the Usenet Archive [260], formerly Deja.com, which lets you search actual discussions for specific text; and the searchable FAQ Index [92].

How do you find newspaper and magazine articles online? Or do you go to the library for those?

I just about never go to the library for an article anymore. Usually I can find what I need online. I may start by looking at Find Articles [98], which provides full text free for about 300 publications, including both popular magazines and medical journals. I may also look at ELibrary [82], which gives subscribers access to the full text of many magazines and newspapers, as well as radio and TV transcripts. Subscriptions are $60 per year. Before I signed up, I tried some searches, which are free, and took their free trial. Northern Light is another site that indexes both free and for-pay articles. Searching is always free.

You can also go directly to individual magazine or newspaper sites, which can be found via links at the *American Journalism Review* [20] site. Some magazines post only the table of contents; others post some or all of the current issue, and maybe old issues too. In general, newspaper articles are free on the day of publication and for a week or so afterwards; archived material usually is not free. But there are many exceptions, and policies change, so it always pays to check.

Medline [162] is the most useful citation index for medical articles. Leading medical journals have Web sites, which are easy to find with a search engine. Google works well for this. Almost all journals provide article abstracts for free, but they often charge to read full text. If I need the full text, I email the author to request a reprint; most oblige.

Do you ever check to see if your own articles are posted online?

Yes, from time to time, I plug my name into a search engine to see what turns up. I also check article databases, as well as magazine and newspaper sites. A few years ago I found fourteen ancient articles of mine in the *Boston Globe* archives, where they had no right to be. I sent a letter to the *Globe* and they took them down.

How big a role does email play in your career as a writer?

Huge! I'm a member of the American Society of Journalists and Authors, which has very active and supportive online communities. I'm in touch with fellow writers via these forums and by email, so I never feel isolated in my home office.

I often send manuscripts to colleagues for comments. Sometimes small groups of us discuss the draft of an article or book chapter via email. When I was working on the early chapters of the lung cancer book, my writer friends told me what was too technical or hard to follow. My expert collaborators couldn't do that, because they know the material too well.

Because email speeds and simplifies communication, new possibilities open. Even if I'm on deadline, I can send a manuscript to a writer friend in Jerusalem for comments. When I was researching smoking cessation methods for the lung cancer book, I read a fascinating article by an Australian anthropologist describing a quitting ceremony performed by elders of a Fiji village. I wanted to ask him a question. In the old days, this would have taken so long that I wouldn't have bothered. But with email, I had his answer the next day.

Email is spontaneous, like conversation—but the words are recorded. I try to remember that when I write. Salon.com published a marvelous article about the "Freudian send" [101], in which the slip of a finger sends your email to exactly the wrong person. I once received such a message. I'd written to a lawyer friend asking if his company could handle a contract matter for me; he passed my message to his boss. By mistake, his boss sent me a copy of his reply, which said that although they didn't have the necessary expertise, they wanted to snare me as a customer. I knew my friend, who's scrupulously honest, would be mortified. So I sent him the Salon article for consolation, with a message: "Tell your boss to reset the defaults on his email software."

Speaking of email precautions: I always check the urban legends page of About.com [4] before I pass along email virus warnings, petitions, and the like. Nearly always, the warnings are hoaxes and the petitions are worthless. But the About.com explanations are invariably fascinating.

Do you subscribe to any electronic newsletters?

I subscribe to lots of them. Some are related to lung cancer or other medical subjects; I also receive e-publications about computers, travel, theater, and consumer affairs. Because all this would clutter up my in-box, I use a free Hotmail [117] account for most of these newsletters.

I find several particularly useful for my writing: Newswise [177] allows journalists to register for email digests of news releases, mostly from universities and academic journals, on science, medicine, business, or life in general. It's a great source for story leads and medical news. Publisher's Lunch [205] has a terrific daily newsletter about book publishing, and a weekly newsletter about recent book deals. The daily mailing often includes links to newspaper articles I might otherwise miss. This week, for example, it mentioned a charming *Washington Post* essay by Dana Milbank, called "It Only Hurts When They Throw Things," about his reactions when his book was panned in the *New York Times*. I saved it in case I ever need to console someone who's gotten a bad review. Publishers Weekly [206] has a daily newsletter aimed at booksellers, with material of interest to authors, too.

What other writing-oriented Web sites do you use?

That depends on what I need at the moment. The premier online resource for books is Bookwire [42], which links to Publishers Weekly and many other industry resources. John Kremer, who's author of the superb *1001 Ways to Market Your Books*, has a Web site [40] with tons of free book-marketing advice and many links to other good resources.

Nolo Press [184] publishes excellent legal self-help books. Its Web site offers numerous articles on topics of interest to writers. I went there recently to get authoritative information on fair use of copyrighted material.

The Guide to Literary Agents [108] helped me last October when I was putting together a book panel for a writers' conference. I wanted to invite a top agent who was receptive to new clients—and I found one. While I was there, I explored the Guide's list of links to agent Web sites. Some of these sites include valuable articles for would-be authors and clients, which made for interesting browsing.

Jim Romenesko's MediaNews [160] has irresistible media gossip, mostly about newspapers and magazines. It's published weekdays on his Web site.

Are you one of those writers who constantly checks her Amazon.com rankings?

I try to keep it under control, but sometimes I can't resist. We had a very strong launch for *Strong Women, Strong Bones*. During one thrilling weekend, when we were ahead of Harry Potter and John Grisham at Amazon, I checked every five minutes. It was fun while it lasted. Most of the time I rely on a free, automated rank monitoring service available from Books and Writers [41]. You give them ISBNs and they automatically email updates hourly, daily, or weekly. I track my own books, and also some competing books, daily.

I see you have a Web site; do you think it's important for writers to have an online presence?

Definitely! At a minimum, it's like having a business card with a portfolio of writing samples attached. But there's potential for a lot more. When Miriam Nelson and I published our first book, *Strong Women Stay Young*, we put up a Web site [239] and started a free monthly e-newsletter to promote it. Our URL was on the book jacket, and we heard from thousands of readers. We loved the "strength training changed my life" letters; reader questions helped guide our revision of *Strong Women Stay Young* in 2000. One of the women featured in our second book—a nurse who weighed over 300 pounds—came to us via the Web site. We joined Amazon's associates program and put links on our site so visitors could easily buy our books—plus, we earned commissions on any sales.

A reader newsletter is a lot of work, but it's a great way to publicize books. We used Mail-list.com [153], which costs $10 a month; their service is excellent and they don't insert ads the way free mailing list services like Yahoo! Groups [278] do.

By the time our second *Strong Women* book came out, we had a mailing list of more than 5,000 readers; the list was over 10,000 for our third book. This gave us big initial sales boosts. I'm no longer involved with the site or the newsletter, but Miriam continues to use them very effectively.

How did you go about designing your personal Web site?

I thought about hiring a designer, but decided I'd rather do it myself. It's like an arts-and-crafts project: Instead of sitting in a rocking chair and knitting an afghan, I sit at my computer and fiddle with HTML tags.

Before I started, I browsed through other author sites to get ideas. The American Society of Journalists and Authors [21] and the Authors Guild [32] have lists of links to members' sites; I also looked at sites on the Random House list [213]. There are many design tutorials online. My favorite is one that teaches good Web design by showing examples of bad Web design; it's called Web Pages That Suck [268].

I used one of the web page templates in Microsoft Word, which I tweaked with an HTML editing program called Arachnophilia [25]. Arachnophilia is "careware," as in "do something positive in the world." As the author explains: "Here is my deal: Stop whining for an hour, a day, a week, your choice, and you will have earned your copy of Arachnophilia." What a deal!

What's your hardware setup? Do you have high-speed Internet access?

My computer is a Dell Pentium II, running Windows 98. Two years ago it was state-of-the-art; now it's an antique. I haven't upgraded because the reports I've seen on Windows 2000 and associated software aren't great, and I'm satisfied with my system. I installed high-speed Internet access—DSL—a year and a half ago. I found good advice about DSL on DSL Reports [80]. My service isn't perfect; there are outages every few weeks and sometimes it slows down. But when it's working properly, I love the speed and the convenience of being connected all the time.

One recently acquired accessory that I find very helpful is a Microsoft Internet keyboard. It has nineteen special buttons across the top that let me navigate online even more easily. For example, I can hit a button to refresh the screen. Another button, and a handy calculator pops up.

What Internet software do you use?

For browsing I use Microsoft Internet Explorer. I have a huge list of "Favorites" that's subdivided into categories so I can easily find useful Web pages again.

All browsers let you select a start page—the page that appears first when you open the program. I use the Yahoo! start page [280], which can be customized in various ways. My personal version gives me health news headlines from Reuters and the AP, as well as general news headlines. If I click on a headline, I get not only the whole wire service story, but, in many cases, links to related stories elsewhere. My start page also has a calendar, search boxes for Yahoo! and for two online telephone directories, links to the local weather report, and links to the package tracking pages of FedEx and Airborne. Yahoo! makes it very easy to select components and arrange them on the screen. For example, by clicking on simple menu options, I put the health news at the top of my page and the package tracking at the very bottom, since I seldom use it.

Another program I rely on is Infoselect [120], a powerful and flexible information manager that lets me save Web pages or other documents and organize them by topics in an outline. When I was researching the lung cancer book, I stashed useful materials in Infoselect, categorizing them by book chapters. The program makes it very easy to move items from one part of the outline to another. When I tinkered with the outline, everything remained in the right subcategory. One of the best features is a super-fast search tool for finding words in saved material. I've begun filing all kinds of easy-to-forget information in Infoselect, such as instructions for dubbing a tape—I do this about once a year and can never remember how. Unfortunately, the documentation for Infoselect leaves a lot to be desired. I haven't had time to wade through it, so I'm not using the program as well as I could. Even so, I find it very valuable.

I wish I were the kind of person who's scrupulous about backing up, but I'm not. Because I keep so much information on my computer, backups are essential. So I subscribe to a service called Connected [61], which automatically backs up most of my hard drive daily in the middle of the night, whether I remember or not. I learned about Connected from Walt Mossberg's personal technology column in the *Wall Street Journal*; the archives are available free online [263]. I love his credo: "You're not a 'dummy,' no matter what those computer books claim. The real dummies are the people who, though technically expert, could not design hardware and software that's usable by normal consumers if their lives depended upon it."

You mentioned that you use the Internet for shopping. Can you give some examples?

Online shopping provides the convenience of catalog shopping, but without all the clutter. Plus, I can compare prices and get terrific deals. An outstanding source of consumer information is Consumer World [62]; some of my best bargains have come via advice and links I found there. For example, Consumer World alerted me to the cheapest magazine subscriptions I've ever seen, many for just $5.95 per year, at a discount magazines site [74]. It also told me about Amazing Bargains [17], a site that gives you the discount codes for zillions of promotions from online stores. I always check there before I buy to see if the store has a special. Sometimes I can get free shipping. If I'm lucky, I'll find a 20 percent-off deal.

Online resources are unbeatable if you're looking for out-of-print or used books. Advanced Book Exchange [9] is a huge network of used book dealers. Last year a friend unexpectedly became the guardian of two teenagers after their parents died. I remembered reading years ago that Kurt Vonnegut's family had lived through a similar experience and that his then-wife had written a book about it. I wanted to buy this book for my friend, but I didn't know the title and I was sure it was out of print. No problem! I went to Google and searched on Kurt Vonnegut; almost immediately, I found a Vonnegut site with a biography that provided his ex-wife's name, Jane Vonnegut. I searched on her name at Abebooks.com, found the book, and ordered it from a bookseller in Virginia. If anyone is curious, it's *Angels Without Wings: A Courageous Family's Triumph Over Tragedy*, by Jane Vonnegut Yarmolinsky, Houghton Mifflin, 1987. All this took less than five minutes. Can you imagine completing such a search without the Internet?

Half.com [111] is like a flea market. The book sellers are mostly individuals; they aren't as scrupulous as dealers in describing the condition of books. Still, it's a great place to pick up bestsellers from a couple of years ago.

This isn't exactly shopping, but I use several inexpensive—sometimes free—Internet-based office services: Big Zoo [36] offers a very cheap prepaid telephone card. I pay less than three cents a minute for calls within the United States; the international rates are similarly low. Tellme [244] is a free information service that's especially handy when traveling. I can dial in toll-free from any location and follow very simple voice menus to get connected to a wide variety of useful numbers: local weather reports and news headlines, taxi services, restaurants, airlines, driving directions, and much more.

Excite [88] offers a free email service with helpful extras. People can send me faxes at a toll-free number and I can view them as graphics files via my Excite email box. I was delighted to have this service recently when my regular fax was broken.

Faxaway [94] lets me send faxes via email. I simply type the message and send it to the ten-digit fax number, whatever it is, @faxaway.com. When one of my book collaborators was in Australia and didn't have email access, I sent her updates via Faxaway; the cost was only about twenty-five cents per page. When I'm traveling with my laptop and staying at a hotel that doesn't have a printer, I sometimes email a fax to myself as a way of printing out a file.

Speaking of travel—do you use the Internet for that too?

The Internet is great for travel information—and travel bargains. Even if I'm planning to buy a guide book or use a travel agent, which I find better for European trips, I do preliminary research online. For example, when my husband and I visited our younger son who was living in Paris, we wanted to stay in his neighborhood. I found a lovely, inexpensive place on a Web site that lists Paris hotels by Metro stop [196]. I thought it would be fun to take a cooking class in Paris. A little Internet exploration turned up the Cordon Bleu site [67]; I made reservations by email to attend a demonstration. That's where I learned the secret of French pastry: vast amounts of butter.

I use lots of other travel sites for various purposes. Consumer World [62] has excellent links for travel bargains. For example, I learned from Consumer World how to sign up for weekly emails with super-low last-minute fares available only online. When I'm looking for a hotel, I go to Quikbook [210] and Hotel Discounts [116], which usually have good rates. But I also check the hotel's own Web site for specials. On my last trip to New York, I saved $20 per night that way. For restaurant reviews in major cities, I check Zagat [282].

For driving directions and maps, I use Mapblast [154] or MapQuest [155]. They draw a map and estimate how long the drive will take. One lesson I learned the hard way is to download driving directions for the return trip, too. I once got lost in Colorado because I relied on Denver-to-Boulder directions when I was driving from Boulder to Denver.

When I'm planning a trip, I often consult the online sites of guidebook series such as Frommer's [102]. Travel magazines are useful too, of course; Concierge.com [60] features material from Conde Nast Traveler. The travel sections of the *New York Times* [182] and the *Washington Post* [265] are particularly good. A wonderful site for women travelers is Journey Woman [137]. I've learned how to stuff a week's wardrobe into a carry-on from the brilliant Travelite FAQ by Lani Teshima [252]. I also subscribe to her free newsletter. My favorite quirky travel site—the kind of thing you'd find only online—is The Budget Traveller's [sic] Guide to Sleeping in Airports [47], with a mind-boggling 1,200-plus listings.

What do you suggest for writers who are just getting started with online research?

Just plunge in. Look around and keep trying new things. Don't expect to become an online research expert in a day; remember how many years it took to develop library research skills. Begin by browsing the indexes at Yahoo!. Or enter a search term—whatever you happen to be working on—at Google. Once you're familiar with those, you can branch out to other search engines.

If you'd rather take a lesson, go to the terrific tutorial put together by librarians at the University of California at Berkeley [257]. They walk you through it: when they suggest a site, they provide a link.

Another good way to learn what's available is to click your way through a good list of links for writers. John Makulowich's excellent compilation is commonly known as The Awesome Journalism List, and for good reason: Officially, it's the Journalism section of the WWW Virtual Library [275]. The *New York Times* also has a superb list of links for reporters [181].

But I believe the best way to learn is to waste time online. Call it background research. You'll find Web sites on almost any subject you can imagine and plenty—trust me—that you'd never think of. For example, I was once discussing urban legends with my kids, and one of them told me, a little hesitantly, that he'd heard what he thought was an urban legend. Suffice it to say that this legend involved Richard Gere, gerbils, and a hospital emergency room visit. Curious, I went online and typed "Gere" and "gerbils" into a search engine. Up popped hundreds of hits. One of them was the astonishing Rectal Foreign Bodies page [216]. Who knew?

The more you explore, the more skilled you'll become at finding what you need. Also—and this is essential—you'll gain a better sense of the extraordinary breadth and depth of available resources. If you don't think to look, you'll never discover the treasures that are at your fingertips.

Super Searcher Power Tips

➤ I have a Google toolbar installed in my browser, so I'm always ready to run a Google search. Google is best for finding the leading sites on a particular topic.

➤ When I needed to find a hotel in Lenox, Massachusetts, I used Yahoo—because it indexes pages by topic; it gave me a tidy list of links to hotels in Lenox.

➤ There's an extraordinary list of specialty search engines at the Leiden University Web site. A less complete but also less overwhelming option is Search IQ.

➤ I find online reference sources particularly handy when I need a tidbit from a reference work I'd never buy, such as a dictionary of symbols or a dictionary of Australian slang.

➤ I just about never go to the library for an article any more. Usually I can find what I need online. Find Articles provides full text free for about 300 publications, including both popular magazines and medical journals.

➤ I often send manuscripts to colleagues for comments. Sometimes small groups of us discuss the draft of an article or book chapter via email.

➤ I subscribe to lots of e-newsletters. Because all this would clutter up my in-box, I use a free Hotmail account for most of them.

➤ When I'm traveling with my laptop and staying at a hotel that doesn't have a printer, I sometimes email a fax to myself as a way of printing out a file.

➤ For a writer, having your own Web site is, at minimum, like having a business card with a portfolio of writing samples attached.

➤ The best way to learn is to waste time online. Call it background research. You'll find Web sites on almost any subject you can imagine and plenty—trust me— that you'd never think of.

Ridley Pearson

Crime Novelist

Ridley Pearson is a nationally bestselling crime novelist. He has crafted fourteen highly praised, frighteningly real thrillers. He has earned a reputation for writing fiction that grasps the imagination, emphasizes unusual crimes and dazzling investigative detail, and, all too often, imitates life. Ridley's novels have helped solve two real-life homicides and settle an environmental lawsuit; his books regularly tackle subjects that eerily become national news after he writes them. These subjects have included the following: the smuggling of Chinese immigrants into the U.S. via cargo containers—undetected in the Northwest prior to his writing of *The First Victim* (1999), now more than twenty such shipping containers have been intercepted by authorities; high-temperature-accelerant arson—a mysterious fire similar to the type Pearson had described in *Beyond Recognition* had perplexed Seattle officials, and at least one death has been attributed to the same type of high-tech arson he wrote about; illegal adoptions involving kidnapped children and the lengths to which couples will go to adopt (*The Pied Piper*); the existence of a crime gene (*Chain of Evidence*); the black marketing of illegally harvested human organs (*The Angel Maker*).

Nearly all of Ridley's novels have at some time been optioned for film. In 1990, Ridley became the first American awarded the Raymond Chandler Fulbright Fellowship in detective fiction at Oxford University. He also gives back to the community: Nonprofit organizations have auctioned off the chance to have one's name appear in a future Pearson novel, raising $20,000 to date; he also volunteers as a teacher's aid in a local alternative school for high school drop-outs and so-called problem students.

Ridley's first love, music, has found expression in everything from writing original folk-rock music for a touring bar band to composing the orchestral score for an internationally award-winning documentary film, *Cattle Drive*. He also plays bass guitar for the Rock Bottom Remainders, a charity fundraising rock band consisting of some of the country's most popular writers, among them Stephen King, Dave Barry, Amy Tan, and Mitch Albom.

email@ridleypearson.com
www.ridleypearson.com

It must be gratifying to hear critics call you "the best thriller writer alive today" and "the most literate and challenging practitioner of mystery fiction at work today." Now let's get down to business. How did you approach the research for *The Pied Piper* and *The First Victim*, two of your books I've just finished reading?

Increasingly, I use a variety of sites on the Internet for my early research. The Internet casts such a broad net around fact that I'm able to specify and identify the particulars well in advance of my field work, saving me time and money.

It's the speed and accessibility of the Internet that boggle the mind. If you devote even a few minutes to a search, you can shave hours off what it used to take you in the library.

Some of the information used in your books is in the physical sciences. In *First Victim*, there is discussion of tides, fish, algae, and marine organisms. In *Piper*, there was talk of pollen and the commercial growing of daffodils.

Much of my physical science research is conducted by interviewing experts. I may collect a great deal of that information beforehand out of articles obtained through Northern Light [185, see Appendix] or LexisNexis [143]. That way I know what I'm talking about, or what I'm hearing.

There are injuries, illness, and cadavers in your stories. Where do you turn for that type of information?

For medical information, I turn either to Dr. Royal McClure, a general practitioner in Sun Valley, Idaho, or to now-retired pathologist, Dr. Donald Reay, formerly the Medical Examiner of King County, Washington. I have also conducted extensive interviews with surgeons, viral specialists, and so on for various projects.

Daphne Matthews, your psychologist-police officer character, helps crack cases with her own special expertise. Where do you go for psychology information?

For psychology, I typically turn to Dr. Christian Harris, a forensic psychologist in the Seattle area with decades of experience. My twist on this is somewhat different. I usually bring Dr. Harris the behavior of my criminals and then ask him to build a background that might justify and explain this behavior. Hopefully, this gives me insight into these characters that I might otherwise have missed.

Your characters utilize digital video cameras, record on CD-ROMs, analyze security systems, and so on. Where do you go for high-tech information?

Most of my high-tech research is done through magazines. Some is a product of the Internet, yes. I try to stay very current with tech developments. One friend, Richard Hart, is constantly sending me articles from Advanced Imaging Magazine [10], which I find fascinating. I've used this information repeatedly.

Did you remember the story of the real Pied Piper of Hamelin, referred to in your book *The Pied Piper*, or did you look it up? Do you consult online reference resources?

Looked it up. I use online dictionaries and encyclopedias constantly now. That's new for me, but for the last year or so I have been doing it that way. I have set my browser to Merriam-Webster Online [164] and then open it whenever I would have previously opened a dictionary or thesaurus. I use them both—and often.

Your books are full of government agencies: FBI, police, prisons, adoption agencies. Are there Web sites you can consult for information on these?

Government sites—they end in ".gov"—are terrific resources on the Web. I've used sites to track bus routes, determine hierarchy within government agencies, track acronyms. These are greatly overlooked and extremely valuable to the writer. They are also a source for identifying public information officers. Public information officers can, and do, answer every and any question a writer can throw at them. One .gov site I used just this morning: A Department of Justice "stalking law" site [256]. I commonly refer to a Washington State government site [266] for the Boldt detective series.

How big a part does email play in your writing career?

I use email constantly. Some of my research sources are in touch with me through email; Dr. Alyn Duxbury, oceanographer, comes to mind. I will email Dr. Duxbury a chapter or two, and he'll read it, or them, and get right back to me with suggested changes.

I also employ an E-Fax [81] account that turns all my faxes into emails so they catch up with me wherever I'm traveling. On our office side, we use WorldCast [271], which is Windows-based bulk emailing software, to keep in contact with the thousands of readers who sign up on my Web site for our newsletter.

What kind of computer setup do you have?

My office operates on Pentium machines running Windows 98. We have three machines, all with full page LCD screens made by Toshiba. The saving grace of the office has been those Toshiba monitors. Now we view full pages, no CRT aiming its photon gun at our eyes. We use HP desktop machines exclusively. We use several brands of laptops: IBM Thinkpad, Digital High Note, Sony Vaio. We use an Ethernet network link, ACT!, the contact-management software, Palm Pilots, and a variety of imaging software. Our two scanners, a Fujitsu and an HP, help us maintain a "virtual" filing system. We try to scan all documents electronically, burn them to CD, and then recycle the paper, reducing storage costs. My assistant, Nancy Litzinger, actually telecommutes to the office; she lives some 2,000 miles away.

Which Web browser do you use?

We use both Netscape and IE5.+ as browsers.

And is your modem connection still through the phone lines?

Yes, I'm still on a regular old 56K connection, using an ISP out of Boise, Idaho, called Micron. I'm promised DSL in the near future. It isn't here yet, and I get impatient for it. Mind you, when I bought my first CPM computer in 1978 I read in the *Wall Street Journal* that only 250,000 personal computers had been sold to date, meaning I was one of those first 250K to own a PC. My first machine had 16K of memory and a 5¼-inch floppy drive, and stored data on a cassette recorder. I wore out the cassette recorder with all my novel writing, and at one point kept it working by shoving a Q-Tip into a slot to trigger the motor mechanism. Colleen Daly, my wife at the time, used to tell stories about how if it hadn't been for Q-Tips I wouldn't be a published author.

My first portable weighed thirty-four pounds, and required early boarding on airplanes. I towed it around airports on a cart. Now I write on an IBM Thinkpad that weighs less than five pounds and is more powerful than my desktop server. Life is good.

Are you a fast and good typist?

I am teased about how fast I type. We've never clocked me, in part because who cares, and in part because I make a lot of mistakes. But I'm fast, yes. However, I once hired a woman named Maida Spaulding who sent back an IBM Selectric typewriter, because she typed so fast it couldn't keep up with her. IBM was fascinated by this. When Maida moved into computers, she had to have a special keyboard buffer, expanded to keep up with her keystrokes.

What are your favorite search engines?

I have recently migrated to Google [104], for speed and accuracy, as a general search engine. I use LexisNexis by phone as my chief research provider, and Northern Light as my Web-based research engine. If you've tried any of these, you don't need to ask why.

On LexisNexis, what type of info are you most often looking for?

I research specific crimes and attempt to determine how common or uncommon they are. For instance, in writing *The Angel Maker*, and having heard that organ harvesting was an urban myth, I turned to LexisNexis, and they produced something like fifty articles, worldwide, dealing with probable cases of illegal organ harvesting. That was enough for me to feel justified in using that subject matter.

Is it from Lexis, the legal service, or Nexis, the business/news service?

You know, we've always just called the 800 number and paid up. I assume it's the Nexis side.

I assume you speak to a professional researcher there?

Yes, we are assigned a researcher who works with keywords that we suggest. As I understand it, each keyword search is additional cost. For instance, again for *The Angel Maker*: "organ harvesting," "illegal organ harvesting," "UNOS," etc. We might have paid for five or six searches. They then fax us a *long* list of articles that produced positive hits. We get a title and a précis of the article, and we select the ones that look to us to offer the most possibility. They then charge us more for the full text of perhaps ten articles we've selected to be faxed to us. We have *never* been disappointed with their results. They are friendly, understanding, and very professional.

Will you ever access LexisNexis online directly?

I'm sure I will. I just haven't yet. We've used the phone/fax method with them for so many years, I just haven't made the switch. They are, in my opinion, the single greatest resource for my research.

Do you use CD-ROMs for research?

We burn our own CD-ROMs and archive research materials that way. I also use mapping software by Delorme [71], which is on CD-ROM. Nearly all other reference material we now use online at various sites. I also use Lucent Technology's Maps On Us Web site [156] for driving instructions.

Are you using the Internet for research for your new book?

I am constantly using the Internet for research. Not a week passes by that either I or my assistants haven't gleaned information off the Web.

Do you ever turn to the public library?

Libraries can't be replaced. I recently flew my assistant to Seattle to spend several days photocopying newspaper articles from the 1880s. Invaluable!

How do your "investigative skills" compare with those of stalwart Lieutenant Lou Boldt, a character in your books?

My character Lou Boldt is an amalgam of the many, many detectives I've interviewed over the years. All have a keen sense of investigation, and all are far smarter than they first strike you. I throw myself into the Boldt role whenever I'm writing a Boldt novel, and later I conduct my research as if I'm Boldt, asking many of the very questions that I've sketched out in my early drafts.

Obviously, two ingredients that go into the making of a successful novel are character development and intriguing plot. Could you comment on the role that information and detail play?

I'm a great believer in fact. When I conduct interviews, I spend at least as much time on the subject's personal and private life as I do on the forensics and particulars. The more you know about a person, the easier it is to fictionalize a character. I'm the guy at the restaurant leaning out of his chair to overhear the conversation going on behind him.

How are the Internet and online communications impacting the work of police and the FBI?

The "FBI and the Internet" is too large a topic to discuss here. There are some serious implications of "raider" programs they've developed recently—privacy issues, and so on. But on the flip side, the criminal world is not lost to the benefits of the anonymity of the Internet. Organized crime is benefiting from the Internet, no question. We'll need to strike a balance, certainly. But I, for one, would not tie the FBI's hands too tightly until we see them misusing our trust. If we do, we put them behind the eight ball before this thing is even off the ground.

Are there any final words you'd like to impart to writers about online research?

One secret to online research is persistence. It's important to read each site's search rules, as they all differ slightly. I wish this would change and we could all agree on a single query system.

Keep trying words that relate to what you're after. Your first choice may not have been the same one used by the person filing the article or indexing the page. Go *deep* into the pages offered by search engines. Your best page may be buried much deeper than you think.

Try many search sites for the same data. I'm constantly amazed how a subject seems dry in one place and then there's an abundance of material available a few sites away. Use the hypertext link offered for "related articles" or "related searches" when you find something useful. This can greatly enhance your search and lessen your time.

When in doubt, head to the library or make a phone call. The best gems are still from the horse's mouth, believe it or not. Nothing will replace a thirty-minute interview with a cop who has spent twenty years investigating brutal murders. Nothing.

Super Searcher Power Tips

➤ I have set my browser to Merriam-Webster Online and then I open it whenever I would have previously opened a dictionary or thesaurus.

➤ I employ an E-Fax account that turns all my faxes into emails—so they catch up with me wherever I'm traveling.

➤   One secret to online research is persistence. It's important to read each site's search rules, as they all differ slightly.

➤   Go *deep* into the pages offered by search engines.

➤   Try many search sites for the same data. A subject seems dry in one place and then there's an abundance of material available a few sites away.

➤   Use the hypertext link offered for "related articles" or "related searches" when you find something useful. This can greatly enhance your search and lessen your time.

➤   When in doubt, make a phone call or head to the library. The best gems are still from the horse's mouth.

David A. Fryxell

Nonfiction Specialist

David A. Fryxell is the nonfiction columnist for *Writer's Digest* magazine [274, see Appendix], as well as Editorial Director for F&W Publications' magazine division, which includes *Writer's Digest*, *The Artist's Magazine*, *I.D.*, and *How*. He is also the founder and editor of F&W's new *Family Tree Magazine* [91], which was named one of the top magazine launches of 1999.

David is the author of two books on writing, *How to Write Fast (While Writing Well)* and *Elements of Article Writing: Structure and Flow*, both published by Writer's Digest Books, and a book of humorous essays, *Double-Parked on Main Street: A Carload of Wit and Humor from America's Heartland*, published by Ex Machina.

Previously, David has been Executive Producer of Twin Cities Sidewalk, an online city guide published by Microsoft; Features Editor, Senior Editor, and Business Editor of the St. Paul Pioneer Press newspaper; Editor of *Milwaukee Magazine*; Director of Publications for the University of Pittsburgh, where he founded Pitt Magazine; columnist for the Dubuque *Telegraph Herald* newspaper; Senior Editor of *Horizon*, the national magazine of the arts; and Managing Editor of *TWA Ambassador* inflight magazine.

David's freelance writing credits include *Travel & Leisure*, *Playboy*, *Reader's Digest*, *American Way*, *AAA World*, *Kiwanis*, and many other magazines. His editing and writing work has won nearly 100 local, national, and international awards.

DavidF@fwpubs.com

You're such a prolific writer—well, you wrote the book on how to write fast—that it was difficult to choose which of your articles to discuss first. I settled on "True North," a piece on finding your Scandinavian roots that appeared in the August 2000 issue of *Family Tree Magazine*. I wonder, was it natural for you to turn to the Internet when you began work on it?

Yes. I'm so familiar with the computer and with the Internet in particular that I naturally turn to it to get a head start on my research. You don't always find all the answers on the Internet, but it does give you a jump start on research. The other reason I turned to the Internet in this case is that so much of this particular topic—genealogy in general—has gone online in recent years.

How did you know that?

From working on the magazine. Also, there had been a lot of media coverage about how, for instance, all the records from the Mormon church went online, and the response was overwhelming and overloaded the servers. This kind of thing was happening and made genealogy more accessible to people. But you shouldn't think, "Well, now I can find my whole family tree on the Internet." It's not that simple yet, although the Internet does make it easier to share and exchange family information.

My article was going to be a "how-to"—what methods readers could use to trace their Scandinavian ancestry. I thought the Internet would be a great starting point for me. I knew that I could find online a lot of experts in the various ancestries I was investigating. The piece was like doing five mini-stories, one for each nationality: Swedish, Icelandic, Danish, Finnish, and Norwegian. I knew that these experts had probably created Web sites or some sort of Internet thing where they were sharing their information. I just had to find them, and then I could take the next step, which was to contact them personally and ask for more specific tips on how my readers could trace their roots.

How exactly did you go about finding these experts?

I went to a few Web sites that I knew would have the addresses, sort of index-type Web sites. But there's one for genealogy in particular called Cyndi's List [68]. I knew about Cyndi's List because of my affiliation with the *Family Tree Magazine* and also because of the publicity it has gotten—she was featured in *Time* magazine, for instance. What Cyndi Howells does—she initially took it on as a one-page project for her local genealogy society and the project grew to gigantic proportions with links to more than 88,000 Web sites now—is catalog and categorize genealogy Web sites. I knew I could go to Cyndi's List and look under Scandinavia and find Web sites where I could get started. It's very much like a Yahoo! [277] for genealogy. Even though it's a very wide ranging site, I knew I could narrow down my search.

Are you ever faced with a writing project where you are forced to go to a search engine cold and just type in a topic word to see what comes up?

Yes. There are two sites I like to go to in those cases. Yahoo! functions like Cyndi's List in that there is some sort of human intelligence behind it, so it's a pretty good starting place for finding Web sites that have at least some relevance, or are more likely to have relevance. It's a better option than tossing a search term out into cyberspace and getting 10,000 hits that you have to wade through.

The other site I like is Google [104] because … well, it just works really well. It also has, in a weird sort of way, a human intelligence behind it. Unlike Yahoo!, it doesn't depend on human beings sitting down and entering Web sites into a database. It rates its results in part on "how often do other Web sites link to this page?" So in a sort of backwards way, it's using a human filter.

For example, if I create a Web site on Norwegian genealogy and put it up on the Web, Google's not going to rank it terribly high at first. But if other sites on Norwegian genealogy discover my page and decide they want to link to Dave's Norwegian Genealogy Page, then the more times they link to me, the more likely my page is going to come up high in the results list when I search on Google. It's completely automated, the way they do it.

I find that Google is more likely to give relevant results. I try to throw in as many relevant words as possible in my search to try to narrow it down. The biggest problem with using a search engine is you get too many results, not too few.

Another example comes to mind. I recently did a timeline on the history of robots for one of our magazines called *I.D.*, short for International Design. Again, I needed to find a lot of information. I wasn't quite sure exactly what information I was looking for, and so I searched Google for words like "robots" and "history." I think I probably did "robots, history, timeline" to try to really get something specific. The ideal hit would have been somebody else's timeline on robots—why not? Actually, I did find a couple of such things, because there are all kinds of fan pages out there. But the key with the timeline, as with the genealogy research, was to find the page or pages that would give me a starting point. I wanted sites that would give me clues that I could then follow up on, because what I started out with was pretty much a blank page.

Hard to imagine you starting out blank.

Well, I could sort of imagine a couple of things I could search on, like Frankenstein. I figured that if I found pages that had "Frankenstein" and "robot" on them, they were more likely to be the sort of historical information I wanted. But I already knew about Frankenstein; I didn't want a bunch of horror movie fan sites. I was looking for something that took it further. What I wanted was something that discussed Frankenstein in the context of the history of robots.

And all the while are you conducting Boolean searches?

Google is, in effect, a Boolean search because you type in the words and the Net finds pages with search term A and B and C. But you don't actually have to type in the connector word AND. Just "frankenstein robots history."

Same thing with Yahoo!?

Pretty much. Because Yahoo! has categories and a hierarchy, if you can find roughly what category you're looking for, then you can go to that category page and find other stuff you might not have hit on.

With Google and Yahoo!, you throw a magnet out and hope that some iron filings stick to it. Then you pull it back, examine the filings, and go from there. But the first step is trying to find someplace to start that doesn't give you 10,000 hits, which is just useless.

So what I'm hearing is, when you are faced with a research project, you turn to the Internet first.

Pretty much. Because it's useful for all kinds of starting points. It might lead to finding an expert, for example. If you're trying to find someone to interview about robots, where do you start with that? If you search the Internet you might find magazine or newspaper articles, and then you find that Professor Hans So-And-So is quoted, and he is a professor of robotics at MIT, and—bingo!—you've got a possible interview.

Have you ever used ProfNet [202], the online service that connects you with university

professors who specialize in the topic you specify?

I've mentioned it and recommended it to people, but I've never used it very heavily. I'm attracted to the more guerilla warfare approach—just seeing what's out there.

Sounds like you enjoy it.

Yeah, it's kinda fun. It's like detective work, in that you try to find leads, and you can kind of build your story piece by piece. And often there's a serendipity factor—you'll discover things you would not have come across normally, just by accident, by looking around.

In the "True North" piece, you mention a few Scandinavian celebrations and anniversaries. Is that how you found that timely information— by accident when looking around on the Net?

Yes, I found out a lot about the whole Leif Erickson celebration thing that was going to take place. I had read somewhere that this was the 1,000th anniversary of Leif Erickson's landing. I probably read it in the *New York Times*. I just casually came across it in some other context as well. There was a museum exhibit at the Smithsonian, so that may have been it.

And then while searching on the Web, I found out about the actual celebrations. I think I found this information on a Newfoundland site. Newfoundland is where they think Leif Erickson landed, where people have excavated; there is a whole controversy over whether he really made it there or not. I was able to follow a trail that led me to the site for the provincial park where these excavations are going on. So I ended up with a piece of information I didn't know going in, and it made a nice lead for the piece because it made it timely—the answer to the question of why do you care about Scandinavian genealogy *now*.

I noticed you mentioned that Stavanger, Norway, was going to celebrate its 175th anniversary. Did you come across this piece of information serendipitously?

That one I did find completely accidentally. I was tracking down sources for Norwegian genealogy and found an immigrant museum or something in Stavanger. When I got to their Web page, here's suddenly all this information. And they're very cooperative and have an English-language Web page. Not only was this site a good resource, but here's this particular news event happening now. That added timeliness, too. I saw it and instantly knew it was something I would use because it was newsworthy and very specific.

Can you imagine, without the Internet, how much paperwork you would have to shuffle through to research an article as jam-packed with information as this Scandinavian genealogy piece?

I can't imagine how I ever could have found something like that without the Internet—unless some other magazine had already reported on it and I happened to come across it reading the *Reader's Guide to Periodical Literature* or something. It would have been excruciatingly difficult to find that, and to delve into detail on a lot of these things.

It also would have been difficult to get a lot of the information right. For the robot timeline, for example, there were a number of things that I knew sort of vaguely—like, okay, I remember the robot from "The Jetsons." But when did "The Jetsons" go on the air? That could have required a lot of work in a library to have found out. I was aware also that there was a robot in the movie *Metropolis,* but I had never actually seen the movie, and I needed to find out the robot's name so I could refer to it.

How did you do that?

I searched first for "Metropolis." Actually, I searched for "Metropolis, Fritz Lang." I mentioned the director's name so I wouldn't get Metropolis, the city in Illinois. I probably also checked the Internet Movie Database [124] site. It's a good starting place for movie stuff, a really huge site about movies. It's got oddball stuff. You could put in "metropolis" and it would tell you instantly what year it was made in. You would know who directed it and who starred in it, all that detail. And I got to—it was sort of peculiar—I got to where I saw the robot referred to as robotrix, but still no name. So then I searched "metropolis robotrix," and turned up pages where I finally found that her name was Maria. I probably used Google for that.

So it sometimes takes multiple steps. A lot of it is a narrowing-down process. The problem with the Web is always that there's too much information out there.

And you're constantly trying to narrow it down.

Trying to winnow down the search, make it narrower. There are two nice things about Google, the Cached and Similar Pages options that you see when you read your hits. "Cached" lets you go back in time to see the actual page as it existed when Google indexed it. That page may have changed, especially if it's a news-type site, a live page on the Internet. If you tried going to the page itself, it might be gone. But hitting Cached lets you go back in time, in effect, and find the page that is of interest to you.

If you click on Similar Pages, you get more pages like the one you hit. Again, it's a good way of narrowing it down. You say to yourself, okay, I cast a wide net and then I found this one that is pretty close to what I'm looking for. Have you got any more like this? And Similar Pages will bring those up. It's really a needle-in-the-haystack thing with the Internet. The odds are pretty high that the piece of information you need is out there, or at least that you can get enough so you can then go to more traditional sources and nail it down.

So you do move on to more traditional sources?

Yes, though it depends on the subject. The best example is probably finding somebody to interview. Once you've found them on the Internet, then you can call them—or email them. It depends on the kind of interview you need. If I need something with some character in it, then I pick up the phone. If I need to sort of probe, if I don't know quite what I need to get from this person, then I'm more inclined to pick up the phone.

If I need very specific stuff, email works pretty well. With the Scandinavia story, once I'd found a couple of experts on each ancestry, I emailed them and asked them three or four very specific questions—such as, what's your number-one tip for someone who's a beginner looking into this? I used email because I didn't need a lot from these people; I didn't have room for a lot! What I was looking for was a couple of good quotes and tips from each person.

The Scandinavia piece probably didn't take you too long to write.

I worked on it on and off for about a month—not full time. If I hadn't had the Internet, it would have been many, many times as much. I saved all my notes. As I found pages, I would resort to the old-fashioned method of printing them out. I've got about a two-inch stack of printouts of the best of the stuff I found. Even then, I only used a fraction of the information.

So the current state of affairs for writers is that we are writing better articles and producing them in a shorter amount of time.

Absolutely. Much more efficient. It used to be that the need for a certain fact could stump you for days. Sometimes it's just that small, stupid fact. I get a lot of those—the small, stupid fact that you really need to know, maybe just an example you want to use. Unless you have the world's greatest reference library in your house, it could take you forever to find that small stupid fact—when was so and so born, or what was the name of the robot? A good site is Britannica.com [85]. I turn to it a lot for the quick "What year was that?" facts because it's a reliable resource. A lot of stuff on the Internet, you don't know how reliable it is.

What's a good rule of thumb for knowing when to trust what you find on the Internet?

You really have to evaluate what sites you trust, what sites you don't. I'll try to cross-check facts. If I don't really know the source of the information, I feel a lot better if I find the same answer on three or four Web sites. On a date, for example, once I've narrowed it down and I've found that, say, *Metropolis* is a 1927 film, I might then do another search. Especially if I found it on some fan's Web page and I'm thinking "Who is this guy?" I would do another search for "metropolis movie 1927" and see if I find it somewhere else.

You have to think about who is behind the Web page.

Yes, because you just don't know. You have to find clues on the site itself to figure out how trustworthy it is. If in doubt, if it's something important, try to double-check it. I feel a lot better if I find a fact in more than one place, as long as it clearly hasn't just been picked up by place number two from place number one. You find that a lot, too—the same piece of information, or quasi-information, just passed around like a virus on the Internet. That still doesn't make it true.

You wrote about getting a fact wrong in print once. You mentioned it in your Nonfiction column in *Writer's Digest*, about how you wrongly attributed the bank-robbing quote,

"Because that's where the money is," to John Dillinger when it was really Willie Sutton.

Oh yes, that! Once I got it wrong—a friend let me know—then I was determined to track it down. It took a lot of looking. That was one of those things that you'd think would be easy, but some fairly obvious-seeming facts turn out to be very complicated. Sometimes it takes a lot of hunting to find a couple of sources that allow you to say, okay, I'm feeling pretty good about this piece of information now.

So it's not a breeze; it's not as easy as we'd like to think.

The temptation is to think "I can find everything right away on the Internet" without doing that winnowing, as well as "I can trust everything I read on the Internet." Both of which are wrong. The Internet is a terrific resource, but it takes a lot of winnowing and it takes a lot of double-checking. It's really the same kind of research skills that you needed fifty years ago as a writer, the same research skills that you would use going to your public library. It's just that the Internet brings the world's largest library to your fingertips.

It's the same kind of skills?

It's the same kind of skills. Following a lead and double-checking information and learning to use primary and secondary sources and all those sorts of things. It's just that it's so much easier now. But the easiness has a downside, too, in that you can get over-whelmed and you can get misinformation.

You mentioned Britannica.com. Do you consult any other online reference sources?

Yes, although in general they're not as good as the old-fashioned way—quotations in particular. The *Bartlett's* you can find online, for example, is something like the 1927 edition. So you know going online for quotations is not satisfactory. For a thesaurus, it's easier for me to use the one that's built into Microsoft Word.

I'd be more inclined to use the Internet when the traditional sources have failed. I've got a big fat *Bartlett's,* and if the quotation's not in there, then I'll try searching for it on the Internet. I'll type in a piece of the quote and try to find it on the Internet because maybe it's out there somewhere. I did that recently with a quote about Oakland. I think it was Gertrude Stein who said "There is no there there." I was pretty sure she had said it, and I was pretty sure she said it about Oakland. But this was information that wasn't necessarily in *Bartlett's*; the quote might be in the book, but not the background of the quote. So, I searched "Gertrude Stein Oakland"—something like that. I was able to confirm it was Oakland. Doing it sort of backwards was a useful way of tackling it.

As for the thesaurus on Microsoft Word, I don't use it often. Sometimes I use it to check on words for headlines or phrases. There's actually a site that is a cliché finder [55]. I wish it were a lot bigger, and in fact I've just discovered a new one that's worth a try [56]. I use these to try to get headline ideas. You know, what phrases come to mind about this subject, with this word, that I can pun something on? You type in, for instance, "chicken" and you get "chickenhearted," "Which came first, the chicken or the egg?," "Choke the chicken," "Tastes like chicken," "Chicken in every pot."

If you are trying to come up with a phrase or a headline or subhead or something like that, you want to avoid clichés on the one hand, but conscious use of clichés—when you can play off of them—can really lighten up your writing. And sometimes it just won't come to you.

You try to think in clichés and you can't.

Exactly.

So you wish the clichés site and the quotations site were fuller and more up to date?

Yes. The more primary reference-type stuff, the really big databases of information that you can get online—it makes such a difference when they're good. That's why I've just sort of adopted the Britannica site; it's one-stop shopping.

I'll use the information in the Infoplease Almanac [119] in somewhat the same way, but usually after Britannica—if I need more "almanacky" stuff.

There's also that Refdesk site [217]. The problem is, it's got too much stuff. It's another gigantic set of links. It's pretty good, but it's overwhelming. I tend to like sites like Britannica where you can just go there, type in what you want to search for, and then get started, rather than having to first figure out "Okay, what kind of source category do I want to search in?"

And Britannica.com is up to date?

Yes. I actually have almost stopped using CD-ROM encyclopedias. I've got Microsoft Encarta sitting on my desk that I've never installed because—well, it's got a few more bells and whistles, but compared to the ease of just going online and finding that information, it's not really worth it. The online version is faster, more up to date. And I don't really need depth from an encyclopedia because, if I'm researching for an article, I'm not going to get what I need from an encyclopedia anyway. I'm going to go way beyond that depth. So the traditional encyclopedia is not very useful except for quick checking of information, and the Web works so great for that.

Do you read magazine articles online?

Yes, magazines and newspapers. I won't read them for pleasure that way, but for work I will. If I'm researching an article, it's great. One tip is, if you find an article and it's long, and you are just looking for a particular little piece, you can do a "Find" on the page. You type in what you're looking for and skip the irrelevant stuff. Go right to it. You save a lot of time. That's particularly useful in searching for genealogy stuff. If you are researching your ancestors and you go to a page that supposedly has something with your family name on it, but there are 4,000 names on the page, you could go blind scrolling through there. When I was doing it, I used "Find" and went straight to Fryxell or Dickinson, which is my mother's name.

How can you find a particular magazine online?

The site I like to go to is American Journalism Review [20]. They have a very good list of newspapers, magazines, and radio and TV stations. They are actually better for newspapers than they are for magazines, but I'll usually start there. They list the publications that have Web sites. With newspapers they are particularly good because they differentiate whether it is available full text, whether it's a daily versus a weekly, whether it's local or covers a major metro area, et cetera.

If you want to check the newspaper in Knoxville, Tennessee, and you don't know that it's called the *News Sentinel*—and the URL isn't NewsSentinel anyway—you can go to newspapers by state, or you can type "Knoxville" in a box, and find out that it's KnoxNews.com.

In their newspaper listings, they break it down so you can look for "full service" or "partial service." The full service is full text, and the partial service is more like ad sites or promotional.

There's a site called PubList [207] that I use to find magazines. It's good for finding the addresses and contact names and so forth.

If you had to read something in a recent issue of *Travel & Leisure*, for instance, are you optimistic that you'd find the full text online?

What you'll get varies so much from magazine to magazine. There are still not that many that will give you the whole magazine online. You've heard, "Why buy the cow if you can get the milk for free?" For most of our magazine sites at F&W Publications, we tend to put highlights up. We don't usually put the whole thing there. It's a business decision the magazine makes.

From a writer's standpoint, wouldn't you like to see all the magazines in full text online?

Boy, it would be great. What you really want is back issues. And that's true for newspapers, too. Those sites where you can search back issues are great. Some charge you for the back issues, and at times it's a little pricey. Sometimes you have to pay for the archives, but you can do the search for free. Sometimes that's worth doing because either you find out that the information is there and then you can decide whether to pay for it, or you find out it's not there, or sometimes all you need to know is what year a story was published and you get lucky—when it turns up, it gives you the date, and you've really found your answer free.

Where do you turn, online and in print, to keep abreast of the latest news about the Internet?

In no particular order: the Wired News site [270]; the *New York Times* [179], especially the Monday Information Industries section and Thursday Circuits section; *PC World*; *PC Magazine*; *Macworld*; *Writer's Digest,* of course, particularly its annual 101 Best Web Sites for Writers issue; and Media Central [159].

Do you check the Web for unauthorized use of your work? What advice do you have for writers who find out their articles are being used on the Net without their permission?

I probably should be more vigilant about this than I am. The truth is, checking is as much ego as self-protection—gee, I wonder how many times my name is mentioned online? Then you discover that some of those "mentions" are people posting your work without permission.

The best bet is simply to use a couple of the better search engines to search for your name—HotBot's [115] advanced search lets you specify that you're searching for a person—and follow up anything that looks suspicious. A couple of times a year is probably sufficient.

You'll also want to spot-check the handful of sites that charge for content. Having your work ripped off by some amateur Web site is bad enough; having somebody else resell it without your permission and without you getting a dime is worse. Some enterprising microfilm companies took it upon themselves to decide that the Web was somehow the same thing and leased their content wholesale. So writers should look for themselves in sites such as Northern Light [185] and Contentville [64] in particular.

Back to Boolean searching. You find you don't need to do it anymore?

It depends on the site. I tend to use just a handful of sites over and over again, because then I don't have to think about it. Like with Google, I'm not even exactly sure what's going on behind the scenes. The home page is just the logo and the blank to fill in your search. There are advanced search preferences and I don't even go to that. I just know that if I type in a bunch of terms that are sort of close to what I'm looking for, I get good results.

How do you determine whether to go to Google or to Yahoo!?

It depends on whether I'm sure there's a page somewhere that's devoted exactly to the topic I'm looking for. For example, I was trying to find the addresses for a whole bunch of tourism departments for individual U.S. states, and I was pretty sure that somewhere out in the Internet world there had to be such a thing already preformatted. I knew if I searched Google, I could find the New Mexico Department of Tourism and then I could find the Arizona Department of Tourism and then I could slowly make my way across the country. But what I really wanted was the "U.S. states addresses page." I was pretty sure there had to be such a thing.

You're pretty optimistic.

Well, yeah. So for that one I went to Yahoo! because I was looking for a particular kind of page that Yahoo! would be likely to have already. And I found a site called "Fiftystates.com" that, although it would take fifty clicks, pretty much had them all in one page. Sometime later, as I was researching the story, I found an even better site that had exactly what I wanted: Tourism Offices Worldwide Directory [251].

So you know from experience which of the two might have what?

Yes. If I'm looking for a Web site, I'm more likely to go to Yahoo!. If I'm looking for a fact or a lead or some piece of information, I'm more likely to go to Google or a similar kind of search engine.

Do you use 411.com [1]?

Yes, although lately I've actually been using 555-1212.com [2].

What about Ask Jeeves [27]?

I've never had very good results with it. I use it, but I find it doesn't quite live up to its promise, which is so seductive. You know, type in a question, it will come back with an answer. It never quite delivers on that promise.

What's your email software?

I just use Outlook, the one that comes with Microsoft Office. It's email and a calendar and that sort of stuff.

Do you have software that organizes the data you retrieve?

Not really. I tend to use more old-fashioned methods like printing out the page. And it's important to turn on the settings in the browser so that it prints out the URL on each page. That way I can later go back and find out what the heck this page was. It's a small thing, but if you don't do that, then you find yourself looking at this great page and saying, "I need to go back there to develop this link, to dig deeper into this site. Hmmmm … I wonder what this page is?"

I do a lot of copying and pasting from Web sites into my word processing program. I'll just copy a chunk of text and paste it into Word. I'll "Select" a chunk of copy, "Copy" it, and "Paste" it into Word. How well that works varies from page to page. Sometimes you get funky formatting. My favorite thing in Word—this is true in Mac and PC—is the Paste Special command. It's on the Edit menu. You pick "Paste Special," and then you pick "Unformatted Text." This makes whatever you're pasting show up as plain text. Otherwise you get gigantic copy, boldfacing, and all kinds of weird stuff. I just want the plain vanilla text.

How are you learning all this stuff? Are you reading your documentation?

Nah. It's trial and error and playing around, and having used a lot of software, and learning things the hard way.

You're a writer *and* a computer geek!

It's true, it's true. I just like to dive in and try it. It won't hurt you. I'm the person in the office—in various offices I've worked at—whom they'll come to with a question before they call the technical people. I'm sort of the in-house unofficial expert. These days it's a really useful ability for a writer to have, because the computer and the Internet have definitely become your tools as a writer.

Does that apply for fiction writers as well?

Yeah. For fiction writers, the research needs are a little bit different, but you end up doing the same thing. What you use the research for is different, but you're still doing research.

Any more search secrets you'd like to share?

My fallback search engine is usually HotBot, but it's exactly the opposite of what I was saying about Google, in that I always use HotBot's advanced search. I never use its regular search. I can't quite explain why, but I think it's because the advanced search will let you do some fairly specific things like search particular domains. You can really get into that narrowing-down process.

With search engines, I don't read the documentation they give you about how to search. I just try it. With HotBot, I've found that it will let you filter by language, region, domain, or date—you can say "any time" or "after" a certain date, or you can pick a specific date. Otherwise you'll get a lot of outdated information for certain kinds of things. And you probably don't really want anything that's more than a year old.

Any other general advice for writers?

Get to know your computer, because it can make your life a lot easier. If you don't know your computer very well, it can make life a lot harder. Don't forget the horror stories of people who've lost files of stuff they were working on. So all those good habits, like backing files up and storing copies in different places, are worthwhile.

So yellow legal pads and manual typewriters are out?

Definitely. You need to get with it. I don't have a lot of patience with people who say, "Well, I'm still doing it on a typewriter and if it was good enough for Hemingway …" You want to be as good a writer as possible and write as much as possible, so why wouldn't you use the tools that help you do that?

Searcher Power Tips

➤   I'm attracted to the guerilla warfare approach—just seeing what's out there.

➤   I find that Google is more likely than most other search engines to give relevant results.

➤   If I don't know quite what I need to get from a person, I'm more inclined to pick up the phone. If I need very specific stuff, email works pretty well.

➤   It used to be that the need for a certain fact could stump you for days. Now I rely on britannica.com.

➤   Sometimes you find the same piece of information—or quasi-information—passed around like a virus on the Internet. That still doesn't make it true.

➤   If you find a long article on the Internet and you are just looking for a particular little piece, do a "Find" on the page. Just type in what you're looking for and skip the irrelevant stuff.

➤   It's really the same kind of research skills that you needed fifty years ago. It's just that the Internet brings the world's largest library to your fingertips. It's so much easier now. But the easiness has a downside, too—you can get overwhelmed and you can get misinformation.

Gregg Sutter
Elmore's Legs

Literary researcher Gregg Sutter was dubbed "Elmore's Legs" in a profile that appeared in the *New Yorker* in 1996. Bestselling crime novelist Elmore Leonard (two of his books were made into movies, *Get Shorty* and *Rum Punch*, which became *Jackie Brown*) doesn't like research but needs it to produce authentic-sounding fiction, and hired Gregg to do it for him.

"Gregg's a super searcher if there ever was one," said Elmore Leonard when contacted about being interviewed for this book. "He's been finding things for me for twenty years. I don't have email. I don't have a computer."

Gregg admits that, for him, turning to the computer is as natural as breathing. He doesn't feel he has exclusive rights to the term "super searcher" because he believes anyone can find information on the Internet.

A native of Detroit, Michigan, Gregg earned a college degree in history. After graduation, he worked in automobile factories and began to make a serious study of the masters of hardboiled suspense and detective fiction.

In 1975, he read his first Elmore Leonard novel, *52 Pick-Up*. He was intrigued by the way Elmore wrote about the milieu of his childhood and made even insignificant streets sound fascinating. Gregg's interest in Leonard's fiction grew, and he finally met the author in 1979. He told Leonard that, if the author ever needed library research, he would be happy to do it.

A year later, Gregg moved back to Detroit and wrote a profile of Leonard for a city magazine. In January 1981, Leonard called him and asked if he would like to do research on the Detroit police. The rest, as they say, is history.

Gregg lives in California now, and his research work has taken him to New Orleans, Atlantic City, Mississippi, Italy, and many other locations. When he's not finding facts for Leonard, Gregg is busy writing a memoir of his years working with the famous author.

The only regret of his chosen work: "I envy people who get to read Elmore's books and have all the thrills. By the time the books are finished, I'm too familiar with the story."

www.greggsutter.com

For Elmore—you call him by his nickname "Dutch"—you take photographs, hunt in used-book stores, and tape-record experts. You also do sleuthing in your local library, but you say you prepare by going online first. Can you explain?

For the kind of work I do, I need to know the volume of available material from the best sources. With a book like *Cuba Libre*, set in Havana in 1898 against the backdrop of the Spanish-American War, I was constantly scouring libraries for mostly nineteenth-century material. Library sources on the Web were invaluable, starting with the Library of Congress [144, see Appendix] and working down to browsing the catalogs of the local library where I would be looking for a particular item.

With this Internet prep, you can walk into a library fully prepared, even check with the library to see if they have the books you're looking for before you make the trip. I am always looking for books on a broad range of subjects, so I check sources like the Library of Congress and Amazon.com or BarnesandNoble.com and see what's out there.

I visited Cuba when *Cuba Libre* was all but finished. I was able to supply Leonard with a detailed description of the Hotel Inglaterra, one of the main locations in the book.

Which search engines do you like?

I basically use three. AltaVista [16], because it has consistently given me the majority of the main sites on a given topic. If it's entertainment or art, I check Yahoo! [277], which yields additional results. Finally, I use Lycos [152] because of its fuzzy search capabilities, to snag some errant sites that haven't been accurately indexed. I have an elaborate procedure of securing the main sites by following links around and making a bookmark list for a particular job.

You have a subscription to Nexis. How does it help?

Nexis [183] is an information source for 2.8 billion searchable articles about news or business. They offer a special subscription for $150 a month with unlimited access to most newspapers, magazines, transcripts, and newsletters. This is my main tool, frankly. The key to this product's use is a careful Boolean search. But since use is unlimited, you can afford to experiment until you get it right. With this tool, I went from fifty percent library time to five percent.

It's expensive, yet reasonably so. It can help any researcher in so many ways. I was looking for the Pomona, California, drag strip and nothing popped up with those terms. I jumped on Nexis and entered the terms and had exactly what I needed in two seconds.

When I first contacted you by phone, you said, "Everything's online. You just have to learn to think in those terms."

It's true. Ten years ago, if I wanted to know something precise or definitive, I had to go to the library. Now, there are many requests that I can fill from resources on the Web, often while Dutch or another client is actually on the phone. There is a cautionary note here, though, because stuff on the Web isn't always accurate or official. But, given the anecdotal nature of much of the material I need, it more often than not serves me well.

How do you handle the possibility that the information may not be trustworthy?

Because information found on the Web may be inaccurate or incomplete, you have to make sure you check it against known sources. I encountered this with Kentucky geology for Dutch's e-novella, *Fire in the Hole,* which is available at Contentville [64]. I needed to positively identify rock formations in a photograph I had taken in Harlan County, Kentucky. I checked online sources against library reference books and phone interviews with mining people in Kentucky.

So anyone researching on the Internet should be careful?

It depends on the type of research. Anecdotal stuff doesn't have to be accurate. But if you have to nail something down, like in the example I just gave, you should cross-check it.

You say that sometimes you're looking for "anecdotal stuff." What do you mean exactly?

For example, Dutch is writing about Harlan, Kentucky, in *Fire in the Hole*. I'm scouting around for anecdotal material on the Web, and I discover a Kentucky recipes page that includes Baked Possum and Fried Squirrel. I knew that was the kind of stuff he liked, so I presented it to him and he used the Baked Possum as an important element in a key scene. I keep an eye out for these kinds of things all the time.

How much use do you make of email?

It was used in an interesting way to get visual information for the writing of *Pagan Babies*. Through a *Detroit Free Press* reporter Dutch and I knew in Zaire, we got in contact with a photographer in Rwanda whose wife was a U.S. diplomat there. We hired him to take pictures of a typical village in Rwanda. I directed his efforts via email, relaying Dutch's requests. From his pictures and detailed maps, Dutch constructed his own Rwandan village as described in the first chapter of *Pagan Babies*. As far as the geography was concerned, we had several maps and guides from both conventional sources and the Web.

How did Dutch find the information he needed about the genocide going on there?

The underpinning for *Pagan Babies* is another book, *We Wish To Inform You That Tomorrow We Will Be Killed With Our Families: Stories from Rwanda* by Philip Gourevitch. This sparked Elmore's interest in Rwanda. It is a chilling account of life and death during the genocide. That gave Dutch all the background he needed.

The Catholic Church figures prominently in *Pagan Babies*. Did you have to hunt for any facts on Catholicism?

Dutch is Catholic. All the Catholic stuff comes directly out of his experiences with missionaries, as explored in his book, *Touch*. He went to Catholic grade school, high school, and college. He knows everything he needs to know. The only things I got for him were some terms for priestly garb.

Characters in *Pagan Babies* drink banana beer. Did you have anything to do with that?

It's in Gourevitch's book. Our man in Rwanda, James Skejskal, shot pictures of guys sucking the beer through straws. An interesting point: Gourevitch talks about guys drinking the beer out of troughs, but James found they only used bottles. Dutch went with the trough because it was more interesting.

The Detroit mob also figures in the book. Did you do any research on them?

I have studied the Detroit mob for a long time. The events Dutch described in *Pagan Babies* were a fictionalized account of the Detroit mob in the mid- and late-'90s. There were reams of articles on Nexis. I typed in "Detroit Mafia." It was as easy as that. And I went to the library to get microfilm copies of photos of houses and mob members. Unfortunately, services like Nexis only give you the text. They do, however, describe the photos that accompany the article. Dutch is very visual and he appreciates when the research is in that form.

What about the part where the characters are transporting cigarettes and risk being caught for tax fraud?

I gave him the facts on that; it's my job. The interesting thing about the cigarette smuggling was that it was a byproduct of another search I had done. And it turned out to be perfect.

Did you find maps and pictures of Rwanda by doing online searches?

Yes. You enter the term "Rwanda" in a search engine and in about five seconds you'll have twenty maps. I was able to find everything I wanted about Rwanda—its government, the history of the genocide, pictures of people, villages—and I even found newsgroups where people are online discussing things like the Rwandan situation. But Dutch got the whole novel out of a few key books and documentaries. A lot of the online stuff, with the exception of a *New York Times* [179] Web-only report on the children of Rwanda, he didn't really use.

Do you have any special software that helps you do things like sort data or manipulate graphics like photos and maps?

My personal software suite consists of Filemaker Pro, Word, and Photoshop. As an example of how I use software, the warden of the Broward Correctional Institute, a medium-security women's prison, told me that the State of Florida, with its Sunshine Laws, has the entire State Department of Corrections database online [100]. This database contained every stat on every inmate in the state.

I wanted to use this data in my research for *Pagan Babies* by creating my own version of the data set in Filemaker. I took raw data from the State of Florida database and saved it as text. I brought the text file into Word, set it up in tab-delimited format. I then imported the file into Filemaker and went to the prison site and dragged all the inmate pictures into the container field for the Filemaker record. There are easier ways of doing database imports with Filemaker 5, but I have always been down and dirty when it comes to data acquisition.

This was a very useful tool because of the Boolean searches I could then perform. I could accomplish several things. I wanted to check out the woman we had interviewed in person, see what was on inmates' sheets, report out searches like "murderers with nothing else on their sheets (man-killers)," and look at the most interesting tattoos and photo reports of all women who dye their hair bright yellow—my custom check field.

What had Dutch's request been regarding this?

He didn't ask me to get him anything. We went to the prison together—can't beat that. I spontaneously began to collect information to have it ready should I need it. I have the freedom in my working relationship with Dutch to collect information that I think he might find interesting. I'm not always collecting information that he specifically asked for.

What's the hardware setup that enables you to be the super searcher that Dutch says you are?

I have a little Mac network in my office. An old PowerMac 7600 that serves as my CD burner platform; a beige G3 tower as server and graphics platform; and, as my main computer, a G3/400 Powerbook with an 80-gigabyte Firewire drive for editing digital video. Also a Palm Pilot, a Rio MP3 player, and soon, an e-book reader.

What browser do you use?

Netscape and Explorer both. Each is buggy, but each has its advantages. Explorer allows you to download Web sites easier, but Netscape seems faster and in some ways easier to use.

Do you have high-speed Net access?

Not yet. I'm still able to function for what I do at 56K. Still evaluating the best way to go. Still concerned about privacy.

Are there any other online searches you've conducted for Dutch that you'd like to share?

I talk to him nearly every day and little things happen spontaneously. Sometimes he may need something during a phone call, like the baseball bat in *Be Cool.* I would then jump on the Web and find out about bats and "sweet spots" and other jargon. I faxed him pictures and he had them during our conversation. That's where the Web is most valuable, in little day-to-day lookups like that. I also use stills, videos, and a lot of conversation to fill out the research. The Internet is just an everyday appliance to me. Isn't it to everybody?

Do you consider yourself a super searcher?

Any ten-year-old who wants to know something will find it on the Web. I am no different from any other searcher except I get paid to do it. I also have a good idea of what Elmore Leonard wants in his research.

Super Searcher Power Tips

➤ Library sources on the Web are invaluable, starting with the Library of Congress and working down to browsing the catalogs of the local library.

➤ I use Lycos for its fuzzy search capabilities, to snag some errant site not accurately indexed.

➤ Nexis is my main tool. The key to this product's use is a careful Boolean search. But since the arrangement I have allows unlimited use, you can afford to experiment until you get it right.

➤ Stuff on the Web isn't always accurate or official. But, given the anecdotal nature of much of the material I need, it more often than not serves me well.

➤ You enter the term "Rwanda" in a search engine and in about five seconds you have twenty maps.

➤ The Internet is just an everyday appliance to me. Isn't it to everybody?

Sheila Bender
Writing Teacher, Poet

Sheila Bender is a poet and writer living in Los Angeles and Port Townsend, Washington. She teaches at Loyola Marymount University in Los Angeles, as well as at writer's conferences and continuing education and for-credit college programs around the West.

Sheila's latest collection of poems is titled *Sustenance: New and Selected Poems*, and her books on writing include *Keeping a Journal You Love*, *A Year in the Life: Journaling for Self-Discovery*, *Writing Personal Poems: Creating Poems from Life Experience*, *Writing Personal Essays: How to Shape Your Life Experiences for the Page*, and *Writing in a New Convertible with the Top Down*, co-authored with Christi Killien.

A founding faculty member of the Colorado Mountain Writer's Workshop, Sheila joins writers and editors each summer for a week of in-residence instruction and readings. She maintains a Web page as a resource for writers. Sheila is also a columnist for *Writer's Digest* magazine.

Sbender1@aol.com
www.sheilabender.com

What's your hardware setup?

I'm working on a Macintosh Powerbook G3, and when I am at home I am hooked up to a cable modem from ATT and Broadband here in LA.

When you turn to your computer to look up a random bit of information, which search engine do you most often use?

I am what my husband, who is in computer networking, calls a "baby user." In other words, I use whatever he has configured my machine to use. That turns out to be Netscape Communicator as a browser and Yahoo! [277, see Appendix] as a search engine. So far Yahoo! usually gets me where I am going, but I do occasionally remember that other engines are out there, and I have used Excite [88]. When I used Yahoo! to find my own home page and it didn't find it, I tried other engines. But now that Yahoo! finds my home page, I stick with it even though I should realize from experience that other engines can be better at finding sites as yet unindexed by Yahoo!.

Out of all the writers I've interviewed for this book—the genres include suspense, historical romance, and journalism—I think your type of writing (personal essays, poetry, writing instruction) requires the least hard-core research. Correct me if I'm wrong. When do you turn to print for answers and when do you turn to online sources?

When I was beginning *A Year in the Life: Journaling for Self-Discovery*, I was working at a two-year college in Port Angeles, Washington. I used that library extensively to locate books on journal keeping so I would know what else was out there and how to shape my book to fill a niche not yet filled. I often used interlibrary loans and the Jefferson County Library as well. Then I moved on to teach for three months in Tucson, Arizona, and I began to need to learn about what healthcare professionals said about journaling. Still, I used print sources I had come across.

Finally, I was in LA where my husband had taken a job after I had signed those teaching contracts, and I was finishing the book. I had decided I wanted to write a chapter on journaling ideas for holidays. He had hooked me up to his cable modem. I began to search for info on the history of holidays and even on what holidays different ethnic groups celebrated. I think that being new in town and not wanting to drive around LA to find libraries, as well as experiencing the speed of the cable modem, pushed me fast into accepting the ease of online research. I also had to write a chapter on resources for journal keepers and checked out the online resources and found information on the Web about off-line resources.

I also often look up books through Amazon.com to see what is published and what people using the books have said about them, just to keep current, myself, about books I'd like to look for or might want to write.

In *A Year in the Life: Journaling for Self-Discovery*, you say you used the Internet to write an appendix geared to inspire or guide readers in writing about specific holidays. Here are the holidays you mentioned; maybe you can remember where you looked for what: New Year's Day, Ramadan, Martin Luther King Day, Valentine's Day, St. Patrick's Day, Passover, April Fools' Day, Easter, Cinco de Mayo, Mother's Day, Memorial Day, Father's Day, Independence Day, Labor Day, Rosh Hashanah, Yom Kippur, Halloween, Thanksgiving, Hanukkah, Christmas, Kwanzaa.

Yes, that's the list. I actually looked up many more holidays than those because I included the solstices and the Ides of March and other famous days of spiritual remembrance. I started with a big book of holidays and their histories from the children's section of the Marina Del Rey Library, which by then I was willing to drive to, having located it close to my husband's new work place. Then I went to the Internet for more info on each holiday. I just typed in keywords using the names of the holidays. I'd use the list of Web sites that appeared from my searches and then use the links on each of these pages to read more.

I just read all the content until the accumulation of information inspired a writing idea for the book. Then I'd condense the information into less than a page and show how my writing ideas came from the information, and also how to use the holiday to spur the writing and how to make up more ideas of one's own. In the end, I had to prune the number of holidays for which I presented writing ideas because the book was getting too big.

When you do research on the Internet, do you worry that the information might not be accurate?

Since I haven't needed "hard-core" facts, I haven't worried too much. I'm looking for springboards and information that will inspire original ideas of my own. When what I read adds to what I've read in print, or is repeated from Web page to Web page, I accept the accuracy.

Regarding the appendix information you mentioned, I also came across individuals' arts-and-crafts and holiday ideas pages. These weren't so interesting to me unless they had snippets of the history of the holidays, but they always had good links.

When I need addresses and phone numbers, I do assume that the Web sites are accurate for the writing organizations I am suggesting people contact, but I usually call myself to make sure that what the pages say the organizations offer is accurate and up to date.

Do you subscribe to any electronic publications?

I put my name on a list from Knopf Publishing [140], which sends me poems from new collections of poetry they are publishing. I like this because I love to read poems and because it alerts me to new collections.

You have a Web site that shows what you do, which is writing and teaching writing. Your site offers links of interest to writers. How did you find these sites?

I find these Web sites in three ways: I browse online myself to see what I might be interested in; I read brochures and newsletters that alert me to Web sites for writers and web sites of literary interest; and people tell me about sites I might want to make a link to.

I try for sites that are easy to use, uncluttered, focused, and, to my way of thinking, very valuable. For example, hearing poets read from their work like you can on the Academy of American Poets Web site [6] is a treasure. The National Association for Poetry Therapy [169] is not as well known as it should be and is easier for people to find, I hope, because of my Web site. Poetry and the Enneagram [200] is a very special site to me. I have studied the Enneagram and went searching online to see what was there and found this site that combines the Enneagram and poetry. I admire the poems that are posted. They are by well-known poets and express the variety of methods of attention among personality types. Clariti [54] is the publication of a colleague of mine. She suggested we link to each other. I like it when writers are generous with information, and Clariti is that kind of site. I add new links every quarter.

How do you feel about electronic publishing, which may be a growing trend—in other words, books that are read onscreen?

I think it is inevitable that most books eventually will be available online, but I sure hope the technology from which we read them gets more comfortable. I don't like reading the screen. I think print-on-demand is an interesting trend, but still uses too many natural resources for the shortages ahead.

Do you ever consult an online dictionary or thesaurus?

I use spellcheck, of course, but I like turning the pages of the real dictionary. I don't usually use a thesaurus. I like to know the root meanings of words rather than other words that mean almost the same thing. To me, words are never really synonyms.

On your Web site, you say you are available as a writing instructor and that the instruction can take place via the online medium.

Right now that means by email. I can receive attachments or memos, and I edit and return them by email. In the future, it may mean interactive and group instruction.

How does email help you in your career?

It makes everything faster, easier, and less obtrusive. I have sub-mitted my last two books by email. That means the usual printer problems I inevitably faced whenever I had to print out a manu-script didn't occur at my house! It means I don't have to wait for the 300 pages to print, then lug them to the copy place and the post office. It means I can start on a new piece of writing instead.

Email also means I am in touch with other writers, my editors, and colleagues without interrupting them. And it means people who want to get in touch with me with a question, a request for instruction, a correction, to give me more information, or to respond to an article or book can do it easily. I love email!

Super Searcher Power Tips

➤ I often look books up online through Amazon.com to see what is published and what people using the books have said about them, just to keep current, myself, about books I'd like to look for or might want to write.

➤ Since I haven't needed "hard-core" facts, I haven't worried too much about accuracy on the Internet. I'm looking for springboards and information that will inspire original ideas of my own.

➤ When what I read adds to what I've read in print, or is repeated from Web page to Web page, I accept the accuracy.

➤ I think it is inevitable that most books will be available online, but I sure hope the technology from which we read gets more comfortable.

➤ Email means I am in touch with other writers, my editors, and colleagues without interrupting them!

➤ Clariti is the publication of a colleague of mine, who suggested that we link to each other. I like it when writers are generous with information, and Clariti is that kind of site.

David Weinberger

High-Tech Topics

Let's hear what David Weinberger has to say about himself. This is lifted (with David's permission) from the last page of *The Cluetrain Manifesto*, the bestselling, groundbreaking book about the Internet and business that he co-authored:

"I hate writing about myself, so here's some minimalist context.

"I taught philosophy for six years at a couple of colleges. Loved my students, felt uncomfortable with my peers. I simultaneously had been writing for a wide variety of magazines, specializing in humor and technology. My writing experience let me move into marketing (thus flipping my philosophical values on their head). Over the years I've worked as a 'strategic marketing' person inside and outside various high-tech companies, some small, some big. I've had the good luck to work with very smart people and businesses from the earliest days of the Web and learned a lot.

"I spend about half my time consulting and the other half writing and speaking about the Web's effect on how we work and live together. I write columns for some magazines, am a commentator on National Public Radio's 'All Things Considered,' and publish my own free zine, JOHO [www.hyperorg.com]. You can reach me at self@evident.com."

In addition to the above, David is contributing a column to *Darwin* magazine and working on a new book to be called *Small Pieces Loosely Joined* (Perseus, Spring 2002).

KMWorld **gives your site JOHO, Journal of the Hyperlinked Organization, a five-star rating. It says: "JOHO combines quality insight and commentary into high-tech topics, market trends, and technologies with unparalleled snarky humor." How do you see JOHO?**

JOHO is my personal zine. I write it and publish it. I do it in part because I write stuff that I, with an author's arrogance, want others to read. But mainly I write it because it keeps me in touch with a very lively, funny, intelligent readership that sends me tons of email packed with links, ideas, criticisms, and jokes.

A very basic question: What's your favorite search engine?

Google [104, see Appendix], of course. It's fast and it spits out highly relevant responses, in large part because it weights sites by how many other sites link to them. You know "voting with your feet?" This is "voting with your link." I use AltaVista [16] when Google isn't giving me what I want because it indexes a heck of a lot of pages. Dogpile [76] looks through dozens of search engine indexes for you. And, on those rare occasions when it's hard to get a search query worded well enough to get good results, I will turn to Ask Jeeves [27]. I use the endangered Deja.com [70] to search through Usenet for discussions of a particular topic.

Since you write about technology, where do you go on the Internet to keep abreast of the Internet?

All over the place. I get daily email newsletters from a few major magazines, including *Internet World*, the *Daily Standard*, and *ComputerWorld*. I really like Keith Dawson's zine, "Tasty Bits from the Technology Front" [243]. It's frequently pretty geeky, but it publishes ideas before almost anyone else has heard them. *KM World* [139] and *Intranet Journal* [127] run information about knowledge management and intranets. Disclosure: I write columns for them. I find out about shareware and tips from Lockergnome [149], an intensely user friendly daily zine. I subscribe to Chris "RageBoy" Locke's quirky screed [212], which is foul-mouthed, psychotic, and indescribably funny. I'm also on a bunch of mailing lists, some of which are private. These lists are frequently the best sources of info around. You can find thousands of them at Topica [250].

What are your favorite general news sources on the Web?

I have a very boring list of general news sources, with a few leftish ones added for spice—and passion and truth: I read the *Boston Globe* every day, but not the other two that I'm "supposed to"—the *New York Times* and the *Wall Street Journal*. Who has time for the *Times,* and the *Journal* acts as if business not only is oh-so-important but is also the final locus of value. To hell with the *Journal.*

I do look at the *Times* on the Web [179], though, and some other sites for news and views: Slate [233], the *Boston Globe*'s Boston.com [43], CNN [59], Reuters [221], the *New Republic* [246], Michael Moore's home page [165], and *Arts & Letters Daily* [26]. And let's not leave out some of the sources of funnier news on the Web: Halfbakery [110], Jim Romenesko's Obscure Store and Reading Room [187], and, of course, the brilliant *Onion* [190].

Want to give some examples of how you use the Internet for research?

I use the Web constantly for research. For example, my newsletter has started running letters from readers about their favorite charities. Someone suggested "The Heifer Project." It took about fifteen seconds to do a search at Google to find sites that confirmed that this is a philanthropy of some standing, although it would take a lot more research to decide if I want to give to it.

Someone else mentioned that he owns the domain www.beefburgerbap.com. Another search at Google, this time on "beef burger bap," came up with a bunch of menu listings that made it clear by context that "bap" is a Britishism for some type of roll or bread.

I also frequently run very short write-ups of enlightened activities that companies are engaged in. I often learn about these companies by reading hard-copy magazines. If they have an online version, as most do, I do a search on that site for some unique words in the article and thus can copy-and-paste quotations, rather than retyping them.

The other day I had written a couple of paragraphs about Martin Heidegger for a book I'm working on. I did my doctoral dissertation on Heidegger, but I haven't paid any attention to the writing about him for the past fifteen years. I wanted to put in a footnote about the fact that he was a Nazi. I did a search on "Heidegger nazi" and immediately found two excellent articles. I spent more time reading them than I'd planned, but I learned a lot and they got me thinking about issues I'd abandoned many years ago.

I also use Merriam-Webster Online [164] frequently as my online dictionary. And there are some excellent sites for tracking down the quotation you want to make sure you get it right, including Quoteland.com [211].

How large a part does email play in your life?

Huge. Most of what I know I learned through email. Because I write a newsletter that publishes a lot of comments from readers, I get a ton of interesting email. People send me links they want to share and arguments they want to start. For example, today I've had a series of exchanges with a guy who read an article of mine and disagrees with something I said about how social we are. It'll probably continue for a day or two, and it will force me to think more clearly. There's also always the vanishingly small chance that I'll actually change my mind. It's been known to happen.

People send me links all the time. For example, after writing a column about why peer-to-peer computing will be important to document management, I heard from three people who say they work for companies that already do P2P document management. The fact that their companies don't really do that doesn't detract from the fact that I've now learned about three companies doing interesting things.

What hardware setup do you have, and do you have high-speed Net access?

Yes, I have a cable modem for Internet access. Currently I have a Dell 600-MHz system with 128 MB of RAM and two hard drives with a total of 30 GB of storage, running Windows 2000. The two drives are important to me because I treat the smaller one as a backup drive. Every day, I back up my document files to it. I also back up periodically to the kids' computer upstairs and to CD-ROM. By the way, the kids currently have a more powerful computer than I. I'm going to have to leapfrog them soon! Why am I so careful about backups? Could a bad experience or two have something to do with it?

I also have a high-end graphics card for gaming, and a 21-inch monitor, which I love because I can see two pages at once. I usually have many, many windows open, so the large monitor makes life much clearer.

I enjoy my Epson Stylus 900 printer. It's faster than I need, but you get spoiled real quickly. I also have an Epson scanner that operates like a copier—one press and a copy pops out of the printer. This only works if you have an Epson printer.

Do you use any special software that helps you with your work?

I use Outlook 2000 and have added about twenty-five rules for automatically moving mail into folders. This helps a lot. I've also written quite a few macros accessible via buttons in Outlook's email windows. The macros do things such as automatically create a new email based on the content of the email sent to me. That's how I manage requests for subscriptions to my newsletter. If the requester has written any type of comment, I respond personally. It's too bad that Outlook's extension language, VBA, is so obscure, because there's a lot you can do with it.

I've also written a whole bunch of programs in Visual Basic—which isn't a tool professionals look kindly upon, but I'm totally an amateur—that do as much of the zine's scut work as possible, such as creating the table of contents and turning email messages into formatted "letters to the editor."

I use AskSam SurfSaver [28] to save Web pages because I want them for research or because they record an online purchase. I like Go!zilla [103] for managing downloads because it lets me schedule downloads and can restart many interrupted ones.

I am currently rebuilding my bookmarks after a "small" computer crash. I now back up my "favorites" file as part of my routine, obsessive-compulsive backup schedule.

This question is a matter of curiosity. You are not a computer science grad, yet you are computer-savvy to a degree that most writers will never reach. Want to tell us how that came about?

I was a typewriter aficionado and owned a succession of used IBM machines when I was in college and graduate school. But spending a month doing nothing but retyping my dissertation took some of the frosting off that particular cake. When then confronted with typing my wife's dissertation, I went to look at one of them new-fangled word processors that Xerox had introduced. As soon as I saw one, I knew I had to have one. Pure lust. So, with the help of my parents, I bought a "portable" Kaypro: an advanced machine with a 5-inch screen running at 2.5 MHz and as much storage as you could fit on a low density 5.25-inch floppy. It was love from the beginning.

For reasons I don't understand, I became fascinated by how the machine worked. How did pressing a key create a character on screen? How did it know how to find a file on a floppy disk? How could an unerase program restore data I thought I'd removed? Because I greatly enjoy listening to conversations that are several rungs over my head, I started reading technical computer magazines like *Byte* and *MicroCornucopia*. Since this is a field, like most, in which to understand anything you have to understand a whole lot, enlightenment came in bursts. After spending many hours and days not understanding anything, I would suddenly understand a big chunk. It felt great.

My excuse for learning how to program was to automate the process of creating end notes in WordStar. I wanted to be able to put the end note information between brackets in the text itself and then use a program to insert the end note number and move the bracketed material to the end. It took me forever to write this program, many times longer than it would have taken me to move the end notes by hand. But it taught me a lot, including the fact that I love the controlled, logical world of programming; possibly by coincidence this was just as I was entering the anarchic world of parenthood.

The next program I wrote was based on my learning that when you do a warm boot of a CP/M machine, it doesn't clear out all of its memory. This meant that if WordStar crashed, you could restart and find the text you'd typed in. But in order to fetch this data, you have to program in assembly language, the lowest level, closest-to-the-machine language there is. This required learning the inner architecture of the operating system, one of those topics that's fascinating if you happen to find it fascinating. I did.

Not surprisingly, having some technical capability—and, more important, some enthusiasm for the technical—helps a lot if you're doing high-tech marketing. It's also surprisingly unusual. The biggest benefit, in my experience, is that you can talk with engineers. Engineers are frequently the smartest people in a company, and often have better ideas about marketing than lots of the marketing folks. Or so it seems to me.

Are writers who aren't Internet-savvy missing out?

There are two big reasons why authors ought to be on the Net. First, if you're writing something that occasionally touches upon the factual world, you can learn more faster on the Web than in the real world. Second, and I think more important, the Web is fundamentally a social place, a conversation. By putting your ideas out—in mailing lists, in a zine, or just in one-to-one email—you get all the benefits of human interaction: new ideas and perspectives, unearthing of assumptions you didn't know you had ... and, of course, an enormous distraction from actually sitting down and writing. The truth is that it almost always takes me until 2 P.M. at least to get through my email and the exchanges it inspires in order to begin working on my book. But my book will be better for it. I hope.

Do you think writers should put up a Web site about themselves, or at least hire someone to do it? Is that kind of self-promotion worthwhile for writers?

If you're writing about what the Web touches, which these days is most everything, then you should get yourself some online experience. Hiring someone to write a Web site about you won't teach you anything except that it's very likely that no one really wants to read a Web site about you. So do it yourself. Get it wrong. Fix it. Try something else. Post the writing that you really care about. Make fun of yourself. Make fun of someone you love. Solicit reaction. Publish the reaction. Make an ass of yourself in public. Get used to it.

What's your stand on e-books and getting

e-published? Most writers are thinking print. Should they revise their thinking?

I am a big believer in e-books. But we're a few years away from their having the readability they'll need to displace a big percentage of printed matter. When we have an e-book with a near-paper-like display for a couple of hundred dollars, people will switch in huge numbers. Reading paper will feel not only old-fashioned and inconvenient, but environmentally intolerable. Sure, there will still be paper books and real bookstores, just like there's still live theatre ... as the exception, not the rule.

Super Searcher Power Tips

➤ Email plays a huge role in my life. Most of what I know I learned through email.

➤ I'm on a bunch of mailing lists. They are frequently the best sources of info around. You can find thousands at Topica.

➤ Hiring someone to write a Web site about you won't teach you anything except that it's very likely that no one really wants to read a Web site about you. So do it yourself.

➤ An excellent site for tracking down that quotation is Quoteland.com.

➤ There are two big reasons why authors ought to be on the Net. First, if you're writing something that occasionally touches upon the factual world, you can learn more faster on the web. Second, and more important, you get all the benefits of human interaction: new ideas and perspectives, unearthing of assumptions ... and, of course, an enormous distraction from actually sitting down and writing.

Reid Goldsborough

Internet Expert

Reid Goldsborough is author of the syndicated "Personal Computing" column, which appears in more than 100 magazines and newspapers throughout North America. He's also author of the book *Straight Talk About the Information Superhighway*, published by Macmillan, and co-author of the 1995, 1996, 1997, 1998, 1999, 2000, and 2001 editions of the Consumer Guide book, *Computer Buying Guide*.

Reid has contributed articles about personal computers and the Internet to such publications as *PC World*, *Internet World*, *Yahoo! Internet Life*, *MSNBC Interactive*, and *Link-Up*. He's a recipient of a national Neal Award for editorial excellence and two Addy Awards for writing and editing.

Before writing full time about computers and the Internet, Reid worked at various other jobs. He was the editor of a photography magazine, director of an air pollution information center, writer for a corporate consulting firm, media director for a political action committee, copywriter for a medical advertising and public relations agency, editor at an optometry magazine, reporter for a community newspaper, researcher for a steel company in Sweden, English teacher in Finland, proofreader of English for a bank in Greece, and laborer on a communal farm in Israel.

reidgold@netaxs.com
http://members.home.net/reidgold

You've said, "I'm a writer who likes to nerd." Which do you lean toward more, writer or computer nerd?

I'm a writer first, nerd second. I'm the kind of person who loves it when the technology works, letting me efficiently do research, submit, and collaborate or shoot the bull with other writers. I'm not a natural troubleshooter, although any time you work with information technology, things inevitably will go wrong, and you do occasionally have to get silicon under your fingernails.

Most people, I think, approach technology as a tool rather than a toy, which is one reason I think what I write resonates with readers. It's not technology for technology's sake, but for our sake. That's why I try to place whatever technology I'm writing about in context by giving it a "what's it all mean?" perspective. Trying to be well-rounded helps with this. I've written about many other subjects besides information technology, including healthcare, politics, history, travel, photography, the environment, and coin collecting, and I try to read widely as well.

Your "Personal Computing" columns are as varied as they are compelling. How do you accumulate the information for all the technology topics you cover?

I keep as up to date as I can by subscribing to all the major print and online computer publications that suit my purposes, including but not limited to, in print, *PC Magazine*, *PC World*, *Macworld*, *Home Office Computing*, and *Link-Up*, and online, daily and weekly news alerts from CNET News [57, see Appendix], PC World.com News [198], and ZDNet News [283].

On a daily basis I clip articles that I may be able to use in the future and file them either physically in a file cabinet or digitally in folders on my hard disk. This is how I come up with column ideas, and it's how I begin research when writing a particular column. I also have a detailed list of information technology experts with expertise in specific areas whom I call for background information and quotes.

One of your columns explored search engines, and you said "a few of them are eminently clickworthy." Want to comment further?

My favorite these days is Google [104]. It's the hottest search engine today, and for good reason. Google uses sophisticated technology that returns site results based on the number of other sites that link to specific information on a site. When key sites, such as CNN.com, link to a site, that's counted more heavily. The end result is an uncanny ability to turn up what you're looking for, and very quickly at that.

With Google's recent purchase of Deja.com, which archives Usenet newsgroup posts, I'll be using it even more. Sometimes searching through the online discussion groups carried by Usenet is a good way of getting a feel for how people in the field regard a particular product, service, or issue.

Do you ever consult print sources?

Despite the timeliness advantage online has over print, print is often a good way to get context and the big picture. It's analogous to daily newspapers versus newsweeklies. Also, the quality of writing is often, though not always, better in print than online.

What do you think about e-publishing?

Online is just so much faster and more efficient than off-line for researching and publishing. You eliminate the physicality of paper. There are those who rhapsodize about paper's history and romance, about how a newspaper or book feels in your hands, and even how it smells. But communicating from one mind to another is what writing and publishing are all about, not the medium through which this communication takes place. Online makes this communication faster, more direct, and more personal.

It's inevitable that more and more publishing will take place online. But I don't see the Internet replacing books, magazines, and newspapers. In the past, whenever a new information or entertainment technology has been introduced, it typically didn't replace existing technologies, just supplemented them. Just as cable TV networks didn't replace broadcast networks, VCRs didn't replace movie theaters, and TV didn't replace radio, the Internet won't replace print. Print, however, will have to adjust and find niches for itself in order to survive and continue to prosper.

How can technophobic writers ease their way into the Internet age?

There are a number of issues involved here. First, everybody becomes comfortable doing things a particular way. Typically, the older we get, the more we resist change. Younger people are more willing, and probably more able, to reprogram their brain's synapses, break old habits, and become more efficient.

Second, many writers consider themselves artists, and artists frequently—though not always—regard technology as cold and machine-like, the antithesis of what's most human. This is a big reason that some writers are, if not technophobic, at least techno-averse.

There's no one way that writers who've avoided the technology so far can conquer it. But it can be conquered, and it should be. Information technology makes you not only a more efficient and productive writer, but also a better writer. It puts tools in your hands that enable you to reach more of your potential.

If I speak glibly about this, it's because I once was technophobic myself. This is one of the reasons I'm still fascinated with information technology today. In my case, my phobia resulted from my getting behind in the one computer programming course I took as an undergrad, forcing me to drop the course. Later, when it came time for me to buy my first personal computer, the bad feelings about this prior experience prevented me from opening the box it came in for three weeks. But once I opened it, I experienced one "Eureka" moment after another, over time, as I discovered how my PC could help me do what I wanted to do. This led to a fascination with the tool, which led me to begin writing about PCs and, later, the online world.

What else do you write about besides technology? Do you ever use ProfNet for any of these other writings?

Along with writing about PCs and the Internet, I've also written lately about healthcare and travel. One big interest of mine right now is collecting early American and ancient coins. I used to collect coins as a kid, and I recently got back into it when visiting a museum with my wife and kids. So I've begun writing about it, primarily from a historical and aesthetic perspective. It's a hobby that helps me stay fresh when writing about my main focus, which remains information technology.

About ProfNet, I've used it more in the past than recently. It can be a useful way to get connected with sources who have expertise in topics you're not familiar with. If it has a negative, it's that the experts may not be the very best in their field, but a lot of times you don't need the best. In my situation though, I have a good list of experts I've already worked with, and it's easy for me to find top people on my own.

Tell us more about your writing about healthcare and travel. How are you doing the research?

I've created a Web site for people with sinus problems. I also sold the content of this Web site to a commercial Web site that sells products for allergy sufferers. And I'll be writing an article for my local newspaper on the same subject, using the same research.

I did research by reading everything I could find on the Web by using common Web search tools, participating in a Usenet newsgroup for sinus patients [232], reading a book on the topic, reading many articles in popular magazines and medical journals, and getting information from medical societies about sinus and allergy problems.

Good general sites about healthcare include drkoop.com [78], MayoClinic.com [158], and InteliHealth [122]. A good site to do research in medical journals is Internet Grateful Med [106].

I've also written for my local newspaper about travel, based on my own travel experiences.

Since you are so widely published, are you ever concerned that someone might be using your articles without permission or attribution? What's the best way for an author to check the Web for unauthorized use of his or her work?

The simplest way to check if others are using your work without permission on the Web is to use a search engine such as Google or a metasearch tool such as ProFusion [203], which uses multiple search engines. This is sometimes called "vanity searching." You type in your name and optionally one or two keywords from a particular article of yours, then check through the hits that turn up. There are free services and pay services that will do this for you automatically, but I've found the quality of the free services lacking and can't justify the expense of the pay services.

Do you subscribe to electronic newsletters and mailing lists? Do you still read a print newspaper?

Each of these brings its own benefits. Electronic newsletters are very timely and can be very specific. Mailing lists, which are online discussions that take place through email, are a way for people with like interests to discuss often very narrow subjects. Print newspapers are still a great way to start the day, letting you quickly scan events and issues of broad interest to society as a whole and home in on those of particular interest to you. I use all three.

What are the best places to find newspaper and magazine articles online?

More and more local newspapers and consumer and special-interest magazines are publishing online versions. Most are free. Some provide the entire contents of the print publication, sometimes time-delayed or with only sample articles to avoid cannibalizing print subscriptions or newsstand sales. You can read the online version of the *New York Times* [179], *USA Today* [258], and *Time* magazine [249].

One good, low-cost way to find articles on specific subjects is Electric Library [82]. You can simultaneously search through 150 full-text newspapers, hundreds of full-text magazines, and two newswires, among other sources.

Do you consult reference works that are either online or on CD-ROM?

The one CD-ROM reference source I use frequently is a dictionary/thesaurus, the American Heritage Talking Dictionary, a product that's no longer being marketed by its developer. But there are a number of similar products on the market that do the same thing. I'm able to look up the definition of a word much faster than reaching for a paper-based dictionary. Also, its thesaurus is more comprehensive than the one in Microsoft Word. And I sometimes use its sound capabilities to have it pronounce out loud a word I'm unfamiliar with, which of course is more helpful in speaking than writing, but still very useful.

The best Web reference site I've found is the Encyclopaedia Britannica site, Britannica.com [85]. It includes the entire contents of the paper-based encyclopedia, for free, and other material as well, including links to relevant magazine articles, news, and discussion forums. Highly recommended.

Do you subscribe to a paid subscription service, like LexisNexis [143]? Should a writer invest in a service like that?

I've reviewed both LexisNexis and Dialog [72]. Although their prices have dropped lately, both services are still priced primarily for business researchers. Still, either may be worth it if, as a writer you're doing heavy-duty research and find other online sources too limited or library research too inconvenient.

How can a writer be sure the info he or she is retrieving from the Internet is accurate?

It's true that the Internet can be chock-full of rumors, gossip, hoaxes, exaggerations, falsehoods, ruses, and scams. But it can also reveal useful, factual information that you'd be hard pressed to find elsewhere as quickly or as inexpensively.

Making sure you're not a victim of info fraud is mostly common sense. Just as you shouldn't judge a book by its cover, don't judge a Web site solely by its appearance. Try to find out who's behind the information at a site. Try to determine the reason the information was posted. Look for the date the information was created or modified. Try to verify the same information elsewhere, particularly if the information is at odds with your previous understanding or if you intend to use it for critical purposes such as an important health, family, or business decision.

What's your hardware setup—and do you have high-speed access to the Internet at this point?

I have one primary work computer and one test computer. The work computer is an aging machine that still serves my research and writing purposes, a 166 MHz Pentium from Micron that has 64 MB of RAM and a 2 GB hard drive. The second machine, which I use to test new software and hardware, is also aging but not quite so ancient. It's a 400 MHz Pentium II from Dell with 128 MB of RAM and an 8 GB hard drive. I've upgraded them both incrementally with hardware and software, but both are about ready to be replaced.

I've got a cable modem attached to one computer and a DSL modem to another. For writers and researchers, high-speed

Internet access, through either cable or DSL service, is much more important than a superfast processor. If you have either available in your area, and you spend any appreciable amount of time online, either is worth the extra money compared with standard dial-up Internet service. You pay a little more than twice as much for about ten times the speed, and the speed increase simply makes going online more efficient and enjoyable.

Is it useful for a writer to have his or her own Web site?

Web sites for writers can be a good way to showcase your writing and your credentials. That's what I use mine for. But most publications still expect you to send in paper clips of your writing when you query them. It's simply quicker for them to look over your stuff this way than to navigate through your Web site.

Do you construct Boolean searches or do you only do free-word searches?

The best advice for building a search query, regardless of the specific search site you're using, is to familiarize yourself with the site's help section first. While there are some similarities among search engines, the differences are such that a minute or two of your time here will make you much more efficient. You'll retrieve more pages that are relevant, and you'll help prevent yourself from having to wade through too many irrelevant pages.

A Boolean search, using terms such as "AND," "OR," "NOT," and "NEAR," can sometimes be useful, depending on the specific search. For example, searching for "dog AND cat" will retrieve only pages that include both of those words. Searching for "dog OR cat" will retrieve pages with either of these words—more pages, total. Searching for "dog NOT hot" will retrieve pages including the word "dog" but not the term "hot dog."

What part does email play in your research and career as a writer?

Email is still the Internet's killer application, despite the flashiness and usefulness of the Web. I submit just about all of my work now through email and converse with editors, sources, and colleagues that way. I still use the phone when appropriate. Email is efficient, but a telephone is more interactive, and it provides more of a personal touch by letting you hear and offer voice inflections and other qualities.

Do you use any special software to organize your email and your downloads from the Web?

I've looked at a number of software programs that purport to help you organize your Web searches and email. But what works best for me is simply storing relevant information as plain text files in carefully organized and labeled folders on my hard disk. It's easy enough for me to find things by eyeballing file names in these folders. Often I'll use Windows' search feature to find specific information within a file when I'm not sure in which file it's located.

With Web searches, I'll typically just copy the text to the Windows clipboard, create a new file using Microsoft Word, and paste the text into the file. Then I save it as a straight text file. With emailed newsletters, I'll typically do the same thing.

Microsoft Word has a useful feature for stripping extraneous formatting and other material from straight text. When you paste, don't simply hit Ctrl-V or go to the Edit menu and select Paste. Instead, go to the Edit menu and select Paste Special and then Unformatted Text. I've created a macro shortcut within Word that lets me do this by hitting Ctrl-Shift-V.

Sometimes—when I want to save an entire email message or Usenet post—instead of copying and pasting, I'll perform a "Save As" within my email program or newsreader program. I use Eudora [87] for email and Agent [11] to read newsgroups.

Have you utilized any image databases on the Internet, such as photos, maps, and other kinds of graphics?

I've used several over the years for varying purposes, but nothing directly related to writing. I've used clipart and photo databases for creating Web sites for myself and others, for creating computer-enhanced photography that I've decorated my house with and given as gifts to others, for creating invitations and greeting cards for myself and others, and so on.

Where do you go for statistics?

I find statistics from various sources: press releases or articles about new studies, phone calls to industry analysts asking if they've done a study on a particular issue lately, and Web sites that collect such statistics. For statistics about computers and the Internet, I've found NUA Internet Surveys [186] especially helpful, along with their emailed newsletter.

Where do you go to keep abreast of the latest in computer news?

The single best source of computer news, I've found, is CNET News. You can read news there at CNET's Web site, or you can direct CNET to email you daily or weekly computer news alerts. CNET also provides other useful computer information services as well, which you can explore at its main site [57]. PC World.com News and ZDNet News provide similar though not quite as extensive services.

How much Internet research did you do for your book *Straight Talk About the Information Superhighway*?

I conducted a great deal of preliminary research over the Internet, as the book was about both the Internet as it was and the Internet as it might become. But I also interviewed key people, including the chairman of the Federal Communications Commission, a House of Representatives committee chairperson, CEOs of several regional Bell operating companies, cable TV companies, and computer hardware companies; the president of CompuServe, the chairperson of the Newspaper Association of America, consumer advocate Ralph Nader, and pop psychologist Dr. Joyce Brothers, about the psychology of using computers and going online. There were people I wanted to talk to but who weren't available to me, such as Vice President Al Gore.

Where do you go on the Internet when you just want to have fun?

I enjoy participating in Usenet newsgroup discussions and email list discussions. I've played a bit with chat rooms, instant messaging programs, videoconferencing, and online gaming but am too busy to spend much time with them regularly.

Have you ever been published in an online publication, or do you have plans to? Would you do the research online to make it a total "online" operation? Do you see this type of total online operation being viable in the future for writers?

I've been published extensively in both online and offline publications. Both publishing and researching online is bound to become even more common in the future than it is today, as a higher and higher percentage of the population goes online. Right now, because of the economics of the Web—people expect information to be free—pay rates are much less for online publications than they are for traditional print publications, on average. But the gap is bound to narrow in the future.

Super Searcher Power Tips

➤ On a daily basis I clip articles that I may be able to use in the future and file them either physically in a file cabinet or digitally in folders on my hard disk. This is how I come up with column ideas, and it's how I begin research when writing a particular column.

➤ Sometimes searching through the online discussion groups carried by Usenet is a good way of getting a feel for how people in the field regard a particular product, service, or issue.

➤ One good, low-cost way to find articles on specific subjects is Electric Library. You can simultaneously search through 150 full-text newspapers, hundreds of full-text magazines, and two newswires, among other sources.

➤ Web sites for writers can be a good way to showcase your writing and your credentials.

➤ Just as cable TV networks didn't replace broadcast networks, VCRs didn't replace movie theaters, and TV didn't replace radio, the Internet won't replace print.

➤ It's true that the Internet can be chock-full of rumors, gossip, hoaxes, exaggerations, falsehoods, ruses, and scams. But it can also reveal useful, factual information that you'd be hard-pressed to find elsewhere as quickly or as inexpensively.

Catherine Coulter

Romance Writer

Catherine Coulter's first novel came out at the end of 1978. It was a Regency romance because, as any published author will tell you, it's best to limit the number of unknowns in a first book, and not only had she grown up reading Georgette Heyer, but she earned her M.A. degree in early 19th century European history.

Following *The Autumn Countess*—a Gothic masquerading as a Regency, she says—Catherine wrote six more Regency romances. Her first long historical appeared in 1982, her "baby," *Devil's Embrace*. She has continued to write long historicals, interspersing them with contemporary suspense novels, beginning with *False Pretenses* in 1988. These days, she writes one contemporary suspense novel and one historical romance each year.

She pioneered the trilogy in historical romance; each of hers is very popular. They include the Song, Star, Magic, Night, Bride, Viking, and Legacy trilogies. She enjoys trilogies because she doesn't have to say goodbye to the characters and neither do the readers.

In 1988, she first appeared on the *New York Times* Bestseller List with *Moonspun Magic*, the third novel in the Magic trilogy. She has continued to hit the *New York Times* Bestseller List—for a total of forty times now—as well as *USA Today*, *Publishers Weekly*, the *Washington Post*, the *Los Angeles Times*, and elsewhere. Well over 37 million copies of her books are in print worldwide.

Catherine's contemporary suspense novel, *Riptide*, came out in hardcover in August 2000 and in paperback in July 2001. Her rereleased romantic suspense books *False Pretenses* and *Beyond Eden* have both hit the *New York Times* Bestseller List for the second time around. Her historical romance *The Scottish Bride*, the final book in the popular Bride series, kicked off 2001 and hit the *New York Times* Bestseller List as well. In August 2001, *Hemlock Bay*, sixth in her FBI suspense series, was released in hardcover.

Catherine lives in Northern California with her physician husband. She loves to hear from readers. You can write to her at P.O. Box 17, Mill Valley, California 94942, or email her at ReadMoi@aol.com. Visit her Web page at www.CatherineCoulter.com.

What hardware do you use?

I work on a Dell computer and I'm on a high-speed DSL connection. I've been working on a computer since 1981. My first was a Vector with 64 KB of RAM. When I updated in 1988, I called the Smithsonian to see if they would like to accept my old computer as a donation. They got back to me saying that if the computer were only four months older, they would take it.

The point is, however, no matter how unsophisticated that little computer was—actually it was quite large and took five-inch floppies that only held about 200 pages of manuscript—it still saved me thirty percent scut work—for example, no retyping a page on my prized electric typewriter when I wanted to rewrite a sentence.

Today, my Dell with Word 2000 and the rest of the Microsoft Office suite still saves thirty percent scut time and gives me, thank God, a very good thesaurus and dictionary.

What search engines do you prefer?

The first search engine I turn to is Google [104, see Appendix]. It's my favorite because I can type in the stupidest thing and it gets me places. I occasionally use Yahoo! [277], although it is not quite as flexible as Google.

When faced with research to do, where do you turn?

For the last five years, when I've had a question, I automatically go to the Internet, not to my own personal library. Why? Because the Internet provides so many more resources than my library. For example, the very first time I used the Internet was when I was writing *The Wild Baron*. I needed to know about the Holy Grail. Within ten minutes I had printed out information from at least twenty sources.

Sometimes I go to Amazon.com [18] and type in the words I'm looking for—for example, "illusion and magic." We're talking bunches of goodies here.

What do you mean by "goodies" at Amazon.com?

I mean that if you type in the words "illusion" and "magic" in the search field, Amazon will bring up a list of books with those words in the title, and these may become good printed resources.

Do you consult online reference resources?

I use the CD-ROM version of the *Encyclopaedia Britannica*. That's loaded onto my computer. What's so neat is that I can simply click on the icon, look up what I want, find it, hit the Close button, and I'm back on my text. On Word 2000, there's an excellent spell checker.

To find quotations, I use books mostly, unless something comes across my path while I'm browsing on the Internet.

Are there any Web sites you can go to to find graphics—photos, drawings, paintings—of a historical nature to help you with your books?

Yes, there are several wonderful Web sites that have color pictures on period costume, for example, that you can print out. Regency Costume [218] has lots of good stuff and good links. Ackerman's Costume Plates [8] is loaded with good information and links.

As for architecture, I have some wonderful books with pictures that have been quite sufficient to date.

Do you have any favorite history sites?

No, I don't have a specific history site that I go to. If I had a specific question, then I'd go to the online *Encyclopaedia Britannica* [85]. If I simply wanted to get more ambience for a certain location at that time, I would go to my personal library and look at my own books.

You sometimes uses foreign phrases in your books. Are there language sites where you can check your spelling?

Any time I use foreign phrases, I use my own books.

Do you find information on weapons on the Internet?

I have two primary books that I use when I need to put a weapon into a book. If you write books that require weapons, then you should invest in your own books.

What about FBI stuff?

On the FBI site [95], you can simply print out everything they provide, which isn't much. In this case, I would strongly recommend print books, such as *Mind Hunter* by John Douglas and Mark Olshaker. The FBI site is helpful, but in terms of really in-depth, sensitive information, you won't find it there. The home page includes some general information and links to other law enforcement-type sites, such as an Interpol Cultural Property Program site [126].

What about finding information on the localities you write about?

For me, it's a combination of using the phone to call local libraries and police stations, using the Net for city maps, and looking at guide books. In *The Edge,* I did go to the city of Salem's Web site [226] and got some maps. To find out the info on the library, which was featured in the book, I called and had them describe it for me so it could be accurate. I have gotten many letters from people in the area who assumed I've visited Salem and the library since I seem to know it so well. The bottom line here is, use whatever you need to use to get specifics.

When you use the Net for maps, where do you go?

We—my researcher and I—often use Yahoo!'s maps [279], or sometimes we go to Google and type in, for example, "map of Anaheim, CA" and Google will give some good choices. We also use Expedia.com [89] for maps.

Do you then print the maps out or just view them on the computer screen?

Yes, we often print maps out. We use a color HP Deskjet printer, which prints beautifully.

Where did you find the mythological references you used in *The Maze*?

That was all done on the Internet. I did this several years ago, so unfortunately I do not remember the Web addresses. There are probably over a zillion by now. You'd just have to go to your search engine and type in "mythology" or other keywords.

You wrote about a computer program named Max that helped an investigator figure out who might have committed the crime. Do you credit the Internet with helping you put that together?

No, I devised Max all by myself using the brain of a nerd friend.

Did you find "Ice acid bomb" info on the Net?

I write fiction. I made this up.

What about military aircraft?

I used a book called *Jane's Aircraft Recognition Guide* to select the MD Apaches for *The Edge*.

The Jane's military magazines have an online presence. Check out www.Janes.com.

We have not used Jane's Web sites. Thanks for making us aware of them.

Did you use the Internet to find information on the rainforest in Costa Rica when writing *The Edge*?

I got that information in several ways. I spoke to a woman who had been in the Costa Rican rainforest. I went to the Internet to get more information on Costa Rica and its rainforest life. And I consulted two or three different travel guidebooks, which are always very helpful. The Web site about the rainforest was neat. I couldn't read it because it was in Spanish, but it had nice photos of flora and fauna, which was what I needed. There is a lot available now in English.

Do you use the Internet for medical information, since people in your books get sick and injured?

I've never been to the Internet for anything medical, for the simple reason that my husband is a physician. I present him with a situation, tell him, "No, I can't take the characters to a hospital, so what would a smart person do?"

Do you consult newspaper and magazine articles to find ideas for the murders in your books?

I have never used newspaper or magazine articles to find murder stories.

Do you read online publications?

I haven't as yet read any online periodicals. To date, I am strictly a print reader.

How does email play a part in your writing career?

I receive quite a lot of fan email because I put my address on my books. This had led to conversations with a sharpshooter from the backwoods of Minnesota who never hesitates to tell me that I've selected the wrong weapon for the job, and conversations with a good half-dozen sheriffs, police, and FBI people who have given me great information. I've never tracked down experts via email, though.

Do you use online bookstores to check reviews of your books?

I never go online to check reviews, particularly such places as Amazon.com.

Does your personal Web site help your career?

I assume that it helps because it allows people to look at my entire backlist, read book excerpts, see all my different publicity photos, some of which are really cool, and enter contests that we occasionally put on.

Is your Web site a way to get feedback on your books?

The Web site is just a good way for readers to find me. The readers who come to the Web site have all been positive.

Do you receive electronic newsletters?

Yes, I receive many e-newsletters that are unsolicited. Since I have so many fan emails to answer per day, I simply delete them without reading them.

Do you make appearances in chat rooms?

I've done chats online with, for example, Barnes & Noble [33] and Microsoft [166]. These live, online chats are usually conducted by a moderator who fields questions and relays them to me on the phone. I answer, the moderator types my answer in for all the people in the "auditorium" to see, and then tells me what they have to say, or asks another question. People ask every kind of question you can think of, but generally I get asked how I got started writing, which is my favorite book, who is my favorite writer, things like that. They type it all in online. It's a lot of fun. I usually do these chats while on book tour. I have also done online chats with book groups in private chat rooms on AOL [24].

Do you subscribe to any online subscription research services like LexisNexis or Dialog?

No, I don't subscribe to any paid services like that.

Do you ever farm out research questions to professional searchers?

No, I don't ever farm out questions to professional online searchers. My personal assistant, Karen Evans, is probably one of the best searchers alive on this planet. If anyone is interested in using her services, let me warn you, she is very expensive!

What's your feeling about writers using the Internet? How important is it for them?

The Internet is a wonderful tool. It's the quickest way to get a "taste" from many different sources. I have found that the more specific your inquiry is, the better luck you'll have finding something useful. For example, asking about the Holy Grail will serve up far more useful results than going in and querying about "religious legends."

The best advice is to use your brain. For example, if you want to find out how a police station in Boston looks, don't go online.

Phone the station in Boston that you're interested in and ask. Get a woman—she will tell you the color of the linoleum in the detectives' bullpen.

Should writers have their own Web sites?

Yes, writers should create Web sites. They are definitely a good marketing tool. They're great places for readers to find out about the author, other books he or she has written, new ones coming up, book tours, and, goodness, anything else the author wants to put out there.

My Web site is taken care of by two wonderful Webmasters, Tom and Diane Potwin, at the *Literary Times* [245].

You've mentioned how your research assistant, Karen Evans, helps you. This last question is for her. Karen, do you have any search tips you'd like to share?

I do a lot of Internet research for all aspects of my job with Catherine—and a lot at home, too, for that matter. Catherine spends a great deal of time on the Internet by herself, but sometimes she asks me to find something for her while she's working directly on her book and needs something pronto.

My biggest tip is that research should never be limited only to the Internet. Libraries still are the best places to get everything you truly need, in my opinion. The Internet is an excellent additional tool but, as any researcher can tell you, you have to learn to narrow your focus to glean the nuggets from the dreck. I must add that patience and following hunches are important, as well, to do good research.

Super Searcher Power Tips

➤ For the last five years, when I've had a question, I automatically go to the Internet, not to my own personal library. Why? Because the Internet provides so many more resources than my library.

➤ The first search engine I turn to is Google. It's my favorite because I can type in the stupidest thing and it gets me places.

➤ Sometimes I go to Amazon.com and type in the words I'm looking for. If you type in the words "illusion" and "magic" in the search field, Amazon will bring up a list of books with those words in the title, and these may become good printed resources.

➤ For maps I use Yahoo! or Expedia.com. Sometimes I go to Google and type in, for example, "map of Anaheim, CA" and Google will give some good choices.

➤ I receive quite a lot of fan email. This had led to conversations with a good half-dozen sheriffs, police, and FBI people who have given me great information.

Michael Gross

Glitz Writer

Michael Gross is recognized as one of America's leading magazine journalists. "Much feared for his razor-like observations, Michael Gross is no stranger to sensational investigative reportage," says nationally syndicated columnist Liz Smith. "Gross turns into an old softie when confronted with the beauty, terror, passion, and pity of a serious true tale. And when he is inspired by his subject, Gross can be as evocative as Proust."

Michael is a contributing writer at *Talk Magazine* and a contributing editor of *Travel & Leisure*. He was previously a contributing editor at *New York* magazine and a senior editor at *George* magazine. His most recent book, *The More Things Change: Why the Baby Boom Won't Fade Away* (formerly titled *My Generation*), was published in March 2000. It has been optioned for development as a mini-series by Gene Simmons, co-founder of Kiss. Michael is currently at work on his next book, a biography of fashion icon Ralph Lauren.

Michael's last book, *Model: The Ugly Business of Beautiful Women*, is the first comprehensive history of the fashion-modeling business. It was a *New York Times* bestseller, a selection of the Quality Paperback Book Club, and is now being developed as a movie for ABC by Columbia TriStar Television.

Earlier, Michael was a columnist for *GQ*, a senior writer at *Esquire*, a contributor to *CBS This Morning*, and a reporter for *The New York Times*. His writing has appeared in *Vanity Fair*, *Interview*, *Details*, *TV Guide*, *Manhattan Inc.*, *Saturday Review*, *Architectural Digest*, *Elle*, *Mademoiselle*, *American Photo*, *Town & Country*, *Cosmopolitan*, the *Washington Post*, the *International Herald Tribune*, the *Village Voice*, the *San Francisco Chronicle*, and the *Chicago Tribune*.

He has profiled such subjects as John F. Kennedy Jr., Greta Garbo, Richard Gere, Alec Baldwin, Madonna, and Ivana Trump, as well as fashion figures Tina Chow, Calvin Klein, Diane von Furstenberg, Isaac Mizrahi, Ralph Lauren, and Steven Meisel. He has written on topics as diverse as plastic surgery, divorce, the A-List, sex in the '90s, and Greenwich Village. For *Travel & Leisure*, he's written about St. Barthelemy, the French Riviera, and Capri.

letters@mgross.com
www.mgross.com

In your book, *The More Things Change: Why the Baby Boom Won't Fade Away*, you chronicle the lives of nineteen baby-boomers who either achieved or failed or both, extravagantly. What part did email play in finding appropriate interviewees, interviewing them, and just generally gathering info about them for this 401-page tome?

I used the Internet throughout the reporting and writing of the book. I did "casting" both on the Internet and using LexisNexis [143, see Appendix], the newspaper database. I found candidates through Web sites and often approached them via email. I set up a network of friends who helped me, also often via email, and I set up interviews with many of the "characters" via email.

Although the interviews themselves were done either face to face or on the phone, many of my follow-ups were conducted by email, as was some of the backup reporting. My favorite anecdote involves Owsley, the LSD manufacturer, whom I found via his Web site [194] and contacted. He emailed back from the Australian outback where he lives. We had a very energetic exchange as he took issue both with the stories told about him by one of my characters, his apprentice Tim Scully, and with many of my notions about the boomer generation. We also used email to set up a meeting when he came to New York. Unfortunately, I left town just before that, so we still have never met.

There's a lot in the book that is "evening news"-oriented. How did the Internet help with finding these old news stories?

Mostly I used Nexis, which is a fee-based database of newspaper articles. My interns—journalism students from New York University mostly—also used microfilm, microfiche, the *Reader's Guide,* newspaper indexes and morgues, and other old-fashioned methods of tracking down information from before the days of digitization. I also keep bookmarks for several dozen research- and reference-oriented Web sites, but find that most of my research is done via Nexis or via libraries. Finally, when research- ing the milieux of my characters, I visited Web sites ranging from those extolling Queer Theory to those condemning left-wing "terrorists."

There is a bibliography in *The More Things Change*, so obviously you used print sources. Should writers be utilizing both print and online?

Online searching has become a necessity, but online sources are not always to be trusted, and old-fashioned library and paper research remains absolutely invaluable. One of the worst things about the Internet is that young people in particular are no longer developing traditional research skills. They are depending on Web sites, and that dependence will inevitably cause errors of fact to be repeated.

So you did consult Web sites often in your research for this book?

I have more than forty Web sites bookmarked in my "boomer" folder.

When you turn to your computer to begin a search for any writing project, which search engine do you log onto?

I'm using Google [104] almost exclusively now. I also make very good use of national phone books, which are available on CD-ROM and now on DVD. They are tremendously helpful when tracking down people whose names are not Smith or Jones.

You wrote an article on Cayo Espanto, in Belize, for *Travel & Leisure*. What did you find on the Internet that wasn't included in brochures or that couldn't be provided by the owner of the resort?

> I found the hotel's Web site before I got a brochure and then was able to contact it via email. I also read up on competing hotels, on the climate and culture of Belize, and on the possibilities for reporting. I did not use electronic reservations, though I have on other trips. And I often check maps and weather online, though the latter is often as inaccurate as weather reports in the daily newspapers.

In the "Alt.Society" article you wrote for *Talk* magazine, there was some information on wealthy entrepreneur Elon Musk, and I wondered where you got it—for instance, Zip2, his community portal for major newspapers that earned him $50 million. Also, his new online bank, x.com, that has attracted $680 million in investment capital.

> I found info on Musk on various e-journalism sites and on Nexis, although he'd already been suggested to me by a savvy cyberfriend via email. I contacted him via a phone number I found on a Web site. I signed up for his PayPal [197] service and tried it, too. PayPal is a way to make and receive payments online. I'm not sure if Musk is still affiliated with the site.

The term "Alt.Society"—where did you come across that?

> I made it up.

For the "Alt.Society" article, did you find information on "old names" and "old money" on the Internet? Did you do searches on Jayne Wrightsman or Sam Peabody or the Van Rensselaers?

No, although their children are often gossiped about on "society" message boards like those on Style.com [240].

Two facts in that article—the sale of Saul and Gayfryd Steinberg's palatial Park Avenue apartment and A. Alfred Taubmon's resignation from the chairmanship of Sotheby's—did you pick these up via online searches?

Nope. Newspapers.

You say in the article that the *Washington Post* and the *Wall Street Journal* have sought to define the class conflict between "appalling new and aghast old wealth." Do you know about these articles from Internet sources?

I hear about them from others, and then read them via their respective Web sites. My current intern had to get me the *Wall Street Journal* piece because she has access to its subscription-only site and I do not.

When you wanted to talk about new wealth, did you type in "Silicon Valley" in a search engine to see what came up?

Nope. It's too broad. Broad searches are time wasters. I looked for specific people, specific companies, and specific accoutrements of the Silicon Valley multimillionaire lifestyle. For instance, I searched for Gulfstream V jets.

What about Steve Kirsch and The Kirsch Foundation? Did you go to the Kirsch Foundation's Web site?

I read about Kirsch in a clip I found on Nexis, then searched him out. But I didn't find his Web site [138] until he pointed me to it. I believe his URLs were briefly not working, and when I told him about the glitch, he immediately fixed them.

Photos of the people you talked about were used in the article. Were these found online?

Yes, but not by me. The *Talk* art department found photos of Kirsch and Musk by going to their own sites and by running search engine searches. You can find photos of socialites, and URLs that lead to more, at Style.com.

You wrote about the psychology aspect of alt.society. Did you use the Internet to find, for example, the Money, Meaning & Choices Institute?

Again, I found out about the institute through previously published articles and subsequently found its Web site [167].

You referred to Ayn Rand's *Atlas Shrugged*. Did you run a search through Amazon.com to refresh your memory? Do you use Amazon and online encyclopedias for that sort of thing?

I buy books on Amazon and I research book titles, author names, and bibliographies there sometimes. I rarely use online encyclopedias because I have a large reference library of my own. That said, when researching particular topics, like Queer Theory, I will often spend hours just surfing the Web looking for sites that can tell me about them.

I judge the veracity of the information based on the source, i.e., a big university Web page posted by a professor is likely more trustworthy than one at a small unknown college posted by a student, which is itself more useful than a Web site posted by an unknown enthusiast. That said, I still check everything with people or sources I trust before reprinting anything I find on the Web.

For the *George* article, "The Lethal Politics of Beauty," did you consult the National Institutes of Health online?

Yes, there is an NIH Web site [172], and yes, I did some research into plastic surgery online. My most memorable experience there was finding streaming video on a surgeon's Web site of a breast augmentation procedure. It was like a car crash—fascinating, yet disgusting.

For this article, did you consult scientific journals online, such as the *New England Journal of Medicine*?

Yes, but I don't really remember finding the journal articles on Web sites. Rather, I got them through Nexis or other pay databases. All the statistics in the piece came straight from the National Clearinghouse of Plastic Surgery Statistics Web site [171].

For this article, you consulted professors: at Rutgers University an evolutionary anthropologist, at the University of Kentucky someone who studies the impact of the media on self-esteem. How did you find them?

I found some of them through ProfNet [202], others through referrals. I do find ProfNet very useful. There is another service that is helpful, too, Direct-PR.com [73]. The service promotes itself as "dedicated to connecting journalists and P.R. folks, directly, at the journalist's urging, and not before." An article in the *New York Times* said the service forwards reporter queries to more than 4,000 publicists.

Regarding the laws governing plastic surgery, which legal sites did you visit?

I got that info through interviews. I have not had much call for legal research. When I do, I try to use Lexis, although some lawsuits and info on them are covered elsewhere online and can be accessed through Web searches.

You mention that you like Nexis and Lexis. Should writers invest in a subscription to them?

Most magazines and newspapers have Nexis accounts, and if you are freelancing for them, they should either give you access or run searches for you. There is now a pay-as-you-go option for Nexis, but I've never used that option myself, so I can't give details.

Finally, I assume you're doing online research for the book you're writing on Ralph Lauren. Care to give any details?

I'm using the Internet constantly in my research for that book. Unfortunately, I cannot share that information right now. You'll just have to interview me again after the book comes out!

Super Searcher Power Tips

➤ To find old newspaper articles, mostly I use Nexis, which is a fee-based database of newspaper articles. My interns also use microfilm, microfiche, the *Reader's Guide*, newspaper indexes and morgues, and other old-fashioned methods. I also keep bookmarks for several dozen research- and reference-oriented Web sites.

➤ If I'm writing about Silicon Valley movers and shakers, I don't type in "Silicon Valley"—that's too broad a search, and broad searches are time wasters. I look for specific people, specific companies, and specific accoutrements of the Silicon Valley multimillionaire lifestyle.

➤ I use Amazon.com not only for buying books but sometimes for researching book titles, author names, and bibliographies.

➤ I find ProfNet very useful for finding experts.

➤ My most memorable experience while researching a plastic surgery piece was finding streaming video on a surgeon's Web site of a breast augmentation procedure. It was like a car crash—fascinating, yet disgusting.

➤ I judge the veracity of information on the Web based on the source. A big university Web page posted by a professor is likely more trustworthy than one at a small unknown college posted by a student, which is itself more useful than a Web site posted by an unknown enthusiast.

➤ I still check everything I find with people or sources I trust before reprinting anything I found on the Web.

Alfred and Emily Glossbrenner

From Bytes to Bios

Alfred and Emily Glossbrenner have been writing for more than twenty-five years. Alfred began shortly after graduating from Princeton in 1972. Among his best-known titles are *The Complete Handbook of Personal Computer Communications: Everything You Need to Go Online with the World*, which was written way back in 1982 and sold close to 200,000 copies; *How to Look It Up Online: Get the Information Edge with Your Personal Computer*, which sold 45,000 copies, and *The Information Broker's Handbook*, which was coauthored by Sue Rugge and sold more than 60,000 copies. Alfred was also the communications columnist for *PC Magazine* and *Home Office Computing* and the shareware columnist for *Computer Shopper*.

Emily joined Alfred in 1990, leaving a successful career at IBM for the vagaries of the writing trade. She quickly became a PC expert, helping Alfred produce books about DOS, Windows 3.1, hard-disk management, and shareware. In 1994, when a graphical World Wide Web had not yet taken the world by storm, they collaborated on *Internet Slick Tricks* for Random House. Command-line FTP is some Net-users' definition of online hell, but they found a way to explain it to readers.

Whether writing about making money or finding a job on the Internet, how to use CompuServe or AOL, personal finance, buying a home, or the art of hitting .300, the Glossbrenners are known for their in-depth research and ability to identify and present the essence of a topic. In all, they have written more than sixty books with combined sales of more than one million copies.

Their most recent title is *About the Author: The Passionate Reader's Guide to the Authors You Love, Including Things You Never Knew, Juicy Bits You'll Want to Know, and Hundreds of Ideas for What to Read Next*. Excerpts and reviews are available at the Web site devoted to the book, www.abouttheauthor.com. Passionate readers themselves for as long as they can remember, Alfred and Emily live and write in a book-filled 1790s farmhouse in Bucks County, Pennsylvania.

gloss@gloss.com

121

Which computers and software equip you to write all these books?

We have three Pentium systems running Windows 2000 Professional. Softwarewise, we have always been Netscape fans. But lately we have found that platform fraying around the edges. Web features that do not work with Netscape 4.7 do work with Internet Explorer 5.5, for example. And Netscape 6 doesn't include one of our favorite features from earlier versions, Print Preview, which IE now has. So we'll probably switch to IE. Bill Gates wins again.

How are you connected online?

Phone lines at a nominal 56K. Cable and DSL connections are not yet available in our area. Drat!

Do you use any CD-ROMs for reference? If so, which ones?

One of our favorites is *Encyclopaedia Britannica CD-2000 Deluxe Edition*, which we've loaded in its entirety onto one of our 20-gig hard drives. But we also subscribe to *Britannica's* [85, see Appendix] online service.

We have followed the information industry since at least 1986, when Alfred wrote *How to Look It Up Online*. It was published by St. Martin's Press and 45,000 copies sold. We have seen companies struggle with the CD versus online challenge. Not that they are mutually exclusive, but the future is clearly online. Why hunt for a CD, which may be out of date, when you can key in a URL and go to a Web site?

That said, the Gale CDs for *Contemporary Authors*, which we used at our local libraries, were invaluable as a source of starting material for many entries in *About the Author*, a fact we acknowledge in the front matter of the book. Although, in all frankness, we found that the quality of the entries varied widely.

I read *About the Author*. Did you consult the Internet to get a list of all the books written by each of your chosen authors? If so, how did you do it?

The general answer is "yes." But we need to add some qualifications. First, whenever practical, we tried to include a list of all the books a given author had/has written, plus announcements of new books yet to be published. But the two-page spread format for each of our 125 authors imposed a discipline on us. When the total number of books written by an author threatened to overwhelm everything else, we opted for a "Best Of" list, based on literary criticism.

To assemble a list of works, we started with standard CD-ROM and print references like *Contemporary Authors* and *A Reader's Guide to Twentieth-Century Authors*. For authors who are still alive and working, we then consulted online book sites like Amazon.com, Barnes & Noble.com, and author-specific web sites. In some cases, we also consulted the Library of Congress Web site [144] for verification of book titles and publication dates.

Did you use the Internet to get the original list of authors, which you eventually pared down to 125? If so, how?

We had three parties contributing their thoughts to the list. First were Alfred and Emily, an English major and a Psychology major, respectively. We came up with a list of some 500 authors who might qualify. We definitely used the Net—after all, by force of habit, we consult the Net for nearly every question—but it was just one of many references.

The other two parties were the book packager, Michael Cader, and Jane Isay, Harcourt's Editor in Chief. They and their staffs had a lot of input on the selection of authors. Together we worked it out. All of us had our favorites; there was a lot of friendly give-and-take, and we ended up with a list of fiction writers that spans history and generations and areas of interest. In truth, all the parties were pleased with the final 125 authors that made it into the book. And to date, no one has said that we should burn in hell for not including some personal favorite.

Did you consult any online or CD-ROM encyclopedias for info on your authors? Did you use any print sources?

The main CD-ROM source we consulted was *Contemporary Authors*, as we mentioned. We were blessed with a cadre of free-lancers, many of whom were associate professors and book editors, and we would send them each a packet of starter information for the authors they had been assigned. The packet would include a printout of the *CA* entry, if one existed, printouts of the Web sites we had found that were devoted to the author, and information we had turned up from other works in our personal reference library.

The freelancers then used their own skills and resources to prepare a first draft of the author entries. They sent us their sources as well as their write-ups, and we verified everything as we cut and shaped the drafts into the final copy.

What was the process of finding out that author Jeffrey Archer's biography *Jeffrey Archer: Stranger Than Fiction* was out of print and then being able to tell readers where to find it?

Our recollection is that we went to Amazon.com [18] and/or BarnesandNoble.com [33] looking for more information and reader reviews for this book. Finding that it was out of print, we checked some of our favorite online sources of used and out-of-print titles—Alibris [14], Bibliofind [35], Powell's [201], and so on. We eventually found it at the Internet Bookshop in the U.K. [123].

How did you find out that there was a "buzz in the chat rooms" speculating about Jean Auel and the writing of her next book? Did you actually visit the chat rooms? Do you ever visit chat rooms for research purposes?

No, we never visit chat rooms. Not that we have not in the past. But we have never found a chat room experience to yield reliable information of any sort. Unless you are a fan of someone or something and you need to do a little antenna rubbing on the subject—and you have nothing better to do—chat rooms are a waste of time from an information-gathering standpoint.

Clearly the freelancer who did the first draft of the Jean Auel entry had a better experience with chat rooms. Some of our free-lancers were very enthusiastic fans of the authors they were writing about, which was fine since this is not a book of criticism but a book about the joy of reading.

Could you tell me about the *New York Times* Books site [180]? It pops up all over your book, and I was wondering how you found out about it and how helpful it is.

We actually found out about this site the old-fashioned way: We read the *New York Times* every day—and the *Wall Street Journal* for balance—and when they introduced this superb site some years ago, they began including a reference to it alongside the book reviews in the daily paper and in the weekly *Book Review* section.

This is a truly wonderful resource for readers. Think about it: You're the *New York Times*. You've got decades of *Book Review* entries and decades of newspaper stories concerning a given author on file. What a great idea to organize and package this information in such an accessible way.

A little personal plug: Our entire writing career has been devoted to explaining things and to directing readers to the "good stuff," regardless of the topic. And if we say it's good, you know that you can believe it, because we have looked at the rest and, frankly, identified the best.

How did you find out about the reading guides posted by Random House [215]?

Publishers Weekly is the leading trade magazine for the publishing industry, so we used their Web site [206] as well as Yahoo! [277] to locate the Web sites of all the leading fiction publishers in the U.S. Then we visited the sites to find out what kinds of resources they offered for readers. Random House was one of several fiction publishers that offer a collection of reading guides for the authors they publish.

I read in your book how the two of you celebrated your 25th wedding anniversary in an Umbrian town and then you read how author Pat Conroy visited the same restaurant you ate at. What's it like writing books together? How do you break up the work?

The two of us have a remarkable level of agreement on the right way to do something—on what information should be included and how it should be presented. From a professional and marital standpoint, we have exceptionally good personal communication, and we have essentially the same tastes. We genuinely like and appreciate the same things.

Certainly there are disagreements at the fringes. But they all get resolved because, God help us, we truly *know* how things should be done. And *About the Author* is the supreme example of that.

I noticed that E. M. Forster has three books on Modern Library's list of the 100 Best Novels of the 20th Century. How did you find the list?

As we recount in our book, this list created quite a stir when it was published in 1998. There were countless articles about it in the *New York Times*, the *New Yorker*, and *Publishers Weekly*, all of which we read on a regular basis. So we found out about the list from traditional print media.

Once we knew of the list's existence, tracking it down on the Net was easy. We knew we could find it in the Books section of the *New York Times*'s web site or at the Random House Modern Library site [214].

E. M. Forster is one of many authors whose public domain works are available as part of the University of Michigan's Humanities Text Initiative. You can download the full text of his books and then you can search the text. How did you find this, and how common is it?

This goes way back in time, but we probably first found the site when doing *Internet 101: A College Student's Guide* for McGraw-Hill back in the mid-1990s. Project Gutenberg [204] and the Online Book Initiative [191] also offer large collections of full-text files of public domain works.

In a sidebar in the section for author James Joyce, you give directions for a search on "Bloomsday" and "James Joyce." You give: "James Joyce" + Bloomsday. How skilled are the two of you at Boolean searches?

We can construct Boolean expressions with the best of them! So why didn't we tell our readers to do a Boolean search for "James Joyce" AND Bloomsday? Most of the popular Internet search engines ignore the Boolean operator AND, requiring instead that you use a plus sign to specify multiple search terms that must be included in your search results. So it just made sense to suggest the plus-sign approach, instead of a Boolean AND, for the James Joyce example.

Your book includes the complete lists of the Nobel and Pulitzer prize winners. How did you approach finding these online?

Online searching has a lot in common with particle physics. Specifically, you know a piece of information almost certainly exists online, even if you have never seen it. Why? Because it's the kind of thing that people would naturally put online. It is impossible to over-emphasize this part of the mental approach to online searching.

When we decided to include the list of Nobel and Pulitzer prize winners for literature, we knew that those lists would be online somewhere. And if they were indeed online, they'd probably be in the Yahoo! directory. So our recollection is that we tried Yahoo! first, searching for "Nobel Prize" and "Pulitzer Prize" to find the home pages. And when they appeared, we felt like physicists viewing a heretofore unknown particle passing through a cloud chamber and leaving an unmistakable wake.

No, it's not foolproof, but this kind of thing happens all the time to dedicated searchers. Beginners stomp up to the door, pound away, and say "I want to find this thing or fact." Seasoned searchers are more like Yoda in Star Wars. The information stream flows through them like The Force, and the threads are constantly moving through their fingers. Really good searchers develop an instinct for this art.

What if you are looking for, say, the Hemingway home page and the title of the home page is something other than "The Hemingway Web Site?" Is just the word "Hemingway" enough?

We found that a title search, which you can do with AltaVista [16] and several other search engines, was often quite effective in turning up official author Web sites and fan pages. But it didn't always work. Other techniques we used to good effect were searching for the author's name in the Yahoo! directory—which we would typically check first, before doing a title search—or searching for the author's name along with the keywords "biography" and "bibliography," since the kind of Web sites we were looking for would usually include sections on the author's life and work labeled with those words.

The bottom line is that if you want to be a successful searcher, you must sit down and think about the query, about the available information sources and their strengths and weaknesses, and so on. You must engage mentally. You must use your imagination, for electronic information retrieval is a creative process. You're a fisherman constantly casting a line, looking for a tug, and reeling it in to cast again in some pool or area of a pond that you think may be more productive.

We used AltaVista and Yahoo! extensively in researching *About the Author*. We like AltaVista because of the size of its database— today, Google [104] is even bigger—and the precision with which we can target a search using Boolean operators, field searching, and date searching. Yahoo! worked well for us because of the selective nature of its directory. We could pretty much count on the fact that if an exceptional author page existed, there was a good chance we'd find it on Yahoo!.

What would you like to say to writers wanting to learn more about searching online?

If you're a writer, whether for profit or for pleasure, you pretty much have to know how to search the Net. The skill of touch-typing is the only one that trumps online searching.

One of the Web sites we consult periodically for an update on what's happening with Internet search engines is Gregg R. Notess's Search Engine Showdown [107]. Danny Sullivan's Search Engine Watch [229] and related email newsletters are also good, but their orientation is more toward Web site creators and Webmasters rather than end-users of search engines.

Another great resource is our own *Search Engines for the World Wide Web: Visual Quickstart Guide*, where we present what we call the "Seven Habits of Highly Effective Web Searchers." We'll give you a summary.

Number one: Develop the Internet habit. When you have a question about anything, check the Net. The answer may lie deep within a company-sponsored Web site, or in a newsgroup posting, or among the millions of listings in a white or yellow pages directory, or somewhere else. But with the right search tool and search strategy, chances are you can find it.

Number two: Use the best tool for the job. For day-to-day searching, you can't go too far wrong with any of the major general-purpose search sites. Our personal favorites are AltaVista, Google, and Yahoo!, but they're not the best tool for every job. For example, if you're looking for recent news articles, forget the search engines and try Electric Library [82]. We pay $60 a year for the service, and it's well worth it.

Number three: Read the instructions. No two search engines work exactly the same way, so it pays to read the online help and search tips provided at the site. For example, some search engines default to doing a Boolean AND search, others to an OR search. Some offer case-sensitive searching, while others ignore case completely.

Number four: Choose unique keywords. Before doing a search, take the time to think about what unique words or phrases are likely to appear in the information you want to find and try them first. To locate sites devoted to impressionist painters, for example, you might try "+Monet +Renoir +Degas," or "Monet AND Renoir AND Degas" if you're using a search engine that allows Boolean operators. That's sure to produce better results than a search for a single keyword like "impressionists" or "painters."

Number five: Use multiple search engines. Every search engine has its own way of doing things, and none of them covers everything. In fact, you may be surprised to learn that even the biggest of the search engines—currently Google at 1.2 billion pages—covers less than half of the Web. So when thoroughness counts, you should plan on using at least two or three search engines.

Number six: Consider the source. Just because it's on the Net doesn't mean the information is either accurate or true. After all, virtually anyone can "publish" anything on the Internet. So be skeptical at all times. Try to determine: What person or organization created the information? What's the motivation behind it? When was the material last updated?

And finally, number seven: Know when to look elsewhere. Don't assume that the Internet contains the sum total of human knowledge. The Net will always surprise you, both with the information that it does contain and with its lack of information on some specific topics. In some cases, your efforts may be better spent getting the information, fact, figure, or whatever you need using conventional printed reference works: almanacs, dictionaries, encyclopedias, and so forth.

Super Searcher Power Tips

➤ The skill of touch-typing is the only one that trumps online searching.

➤ Online searching has a lot in common with particle physics. You know a piece of information almost certainly exists online, even if you have never seen it. But don't assume that the Internet contains the sum total of human knowledge.

➤ Our favorite online sources of used and out-of-print titles are Alibris, Bibliofind, and Powell's.

➤ Virtually anyone can "publish" anything on the Internet. So be skeptical at all times.

➤ If you want to be a successful searcher, you must sit down and think about the query, about the available information sources and their strengths and weaknesses. You must engage mentally. You must use your imagination, for electronic information retrieval is a creative process.

Bonnie Kohn Remsberg

Dramatic Narratives and Scriptwriting

In a thirty-five-year journalism career, Bonnie Kohn Remsberg has written more than a thousand dramatic narratives and articles for *Reader's Digest*, *Family Circle*, *Ladies' Home Journal*, *Woman's Day*, *Redbook*, *Good Housekeeping*, *Seventeen*, *Playboy*, *Esquire*, *Saturday Review*, the *New York Times Magazine*, *Success*, *Consumer Reports*, *Catholic Digest*, the *World Book Encyclopedia Yearbook*, and other publications.

Her books include *Mom, Dad, Mike and Pattie: The True Story of the Columbo Murders*, a Main Selection of the True Crime Book Club, optioned by Republic Pictures; *The Stress-Proof Child: A Loving Parent's Guide* (co-author); and *Radio and TV Spot Announcements for Family Planning, Community and Family Study Center*, distributed by the United Nations and the Ford Foundation to developing countries. Its scripts, translated into more than twenty languages, are in production in dozens of countries.

Bonnie's work appears in numerous anthologies, including the acclaimed *Smiling Through the Apocalypse: Esquire's History of the '60s* (reissued 1987), and *The Complete Guide to Writing Non-Fiction* by the American Society of Journalists and Authors (ASJA). She has also reviewed books for the *Washington Post*, the *Chicago Sun-Times*, and the *Cleveland Plain Dealer*.

Bonnie has written many award-winning films and television documentaries, including *Karen Anne*, the docudrama on the historic Karen Anne Quinlan right-to-die case for Westinghouse Broadcasting.

She has won the ASJA Outstanding Magazine Article Award, the Sidney Hillman Award for Outstanding Article on a Social Issue, and, twice, the Penney-Missouri Award for women's-interest journalism. *The Art of Writing Non-Fiction* cites her as a modern writer who keeps the public informed "in the tradition of Samuel Adams, Tom Paine, Ida M. Tarbell, and Woodward and Bernstein."

Bonnie is the biological mother of two, foster mother of two, stepmother of four, and grandmother of four.

BonnieRemsberg@compuserve.com

You're a writer of diverse talents—nonfiction writer, scriptwriter, dramatist. Your career blows me away. Could you tell us about the play writing you're doing now?

I started out in life in puppetry and theater, then got side-tracked onto journalism which, good-news-bad-news joke, I turned out to be good at. There comes a time in everyone's life, however, when you realize that you're not going to live forever and if you expect to make your childhood dreams come true, you better get at it.

Mine came with the death of a close friend. Knowing she would want me to, I went back to the theater, now as an experienced writer with a lot of typing under my belt. I'm writing plays in which characters are portrayed by puppets who were, in their lives, puppets for whatever reason. The world of adult puppet theater is astoundingly interesting, creative, and exciting. I haven't regretted a second of it.

My play *The Whaling Wife*, which premiered in Ohio in 1997, is based on the journals and diaries of the women who accompanied their whaling captain husbands on three- to four-year voyages in the mid-1800s. The lead character, Sarah, is a puppet. My current play, *Fireball*, is the story of a man who was caught up in the largest criminal investigation of judicial corruption in the nation's history, the Greylord scandal in Chicago. The character of the political machine of Mayor Richard J. Daley is a giant puppet. The lead character, a judge, is a puppet.

Ideas for plays come from everywhere. Finding ideas has never been a problem. Finding time for all the ideas is the challenge.

Now, about online searching. You have told me that you make some use of the Internet and that you have uncovered interesting stuff. First of all, what's the search engine you instinctively reach for when you need a piece

of information? We'll get to the "interesting stuff" later.

My favorite search engine is ixquick [131, see Appendix]. I learned about it from a fellow ASJA member, and I find it much more comprehensive and less nonsensical than most of them. My second favorite is Dogpile [76]. Both are compilation searches, so you get to look into a whole assortment of data collections. Still, I find that no matter how good the engine is, there's a great amount of irrelevant material. It's still a search, even with all that help.

What do you do about the "irrelevant material" problem?

The only way I've found to deal with irrelevant material is to avoid it, if possible. So I make guesses about what is turning up on a search engine and use my judgment. I don't always guess right, so I try to get away from the clearly off-the-path stuff as fast as possible. I'm migraine-prone, so I almost automatically know that when I get into something with flashing lights and stuff bouncing around, it's not only irrelevant, it's harmful. That I avoid like the plague. I think that sooner or later the Web will have to deal with this problem. I'm not the only person subject to harm from flashing lights. And so many people seem to feel that the more glitzy they make their site, the better it is. In my opinion, the opposite is true.

Did you use the Internet at all for the writing of *Mom, Dad, Mike, and Pattie: The True Story of the Columbo Murders*?

M,D,M&P preceded the Internet, or at least my entry into it. I used the old-fashioned techniques in researching that book— shoe leather and iron-butt interviews. Actually, I don't think the Internet would have changed anything. That story came largely from cops, relatives, courtroom attendance, and prison visits. None would have been on the Internet.

What role does email play in your writing career?

Writing, as I'm sure everybody knows by now, is a lonely business. This is the good news and the bad news. Since the advent of email, I find I can connect socially with people without that interfering with my work time. It is the most controllable socialization I can imagine. I love it. The downside is being bombarded with email press releases, which have to be deleted at the beginning of the day.

Has email helped you in making contacts and interviewing people?

Email is enormously effective for making arrangements, exchanging factual material—like arrival and departure times for trips and so on, when someone is meeting you—but I still prefer the telephone for anything that may lead to a chat.

I've always found face-to-face interviews more productive than flat surfaces. Most of my magazine articles were what they call in the biz "ordeals"—a family or an individual who has gone through an intense experience and is more or less willing to share it. These interviews were all conducted at kitchen tables, or similar intimate spots.

Once, I did a story about a beaten wife who ended up killing her husband and, amazingly, being acquitted. She did not want to talk to me; her lawyer convinced her to. She wouldn't let me in her house, would only agree to come to my motel room. Then she was reticent. The interview was like pulling teeth, but I persevered. As she got up to leave, she stood at the door and said, "Sometimes at night, he comes to me in dreams. He is sweet again, and we're happy. Then I wake up crying." Now, do you honestly think that all the email in the world, or even a telephone, for that matter, would have allowed me to get that?

But don't you agree that the Internet—which includes email, forums, chat rooms, and Web sites—enables us to make contact with people we may not otherwise have had the opportunity to exchange words with?

I have contacts with people online, but I cannot really think of any—except for a few ASJA members—that I wasn't already in contact with going in. I think email is a great way to keep in touch with people but I already have the people. For example, I have two kids who live in the Orient—one in Japan, one in Singapore. Telephone calls, which we do occasionally, are expensive. So we rely on email all the time. It's wonderful.

You have quite a list of magazine credits. Could you tell us if the Internet helped with the research for any of them?

No, the Internet did not figure in any of these stories, all of which preceded it. My articles were personal stories, mostly family centered, ranging from the bizarre to the criminal to the tragic. I spent much of my magazine writing career in tears. And, by the way, I always knew that if I was sitting at the keyboard weeping, I was probably getting it right. When you do that kind of work, you have to filter the emotions through your own emotional base. If you don't have one, don't bother to try.

Do you ever have to consult the Internet for writing a play?

I have consulted the Internet in writing my plays, but, again, the old-fashioned research techniques have proved most productive. *The Whaling Wife* leaned heavily on research material from the 19th century. Not on the Internet. My current play is, again, based on historical material that happened in the 1970s and '80s. Most of that stuff isn't on the Web.

Where do you turn to find articles online?

Major newspapers. My present play is set in Chicago. The *Tribune* [52] and the *Sun-Times* [51] have been helpful. I use the *Washington Post* [264] from time to time.

I find online newspapers useful for current stuff. But most don't archive past a couple of weeks or so. So real digging still gets done the old-fashioned way. Also, so many of them charge for each article you download that it could get expensive to go on fishing trips.

Do you use online or CD-ROM reference resources, like a dictionary, thesaurus, encyclopedia, or collection of quotations?

I use the dictionary in my word-processing program, but other than that, I'm an old-fashioned girl with an array of reference books, well thumbed. One of my favorites is *Webster's New World Word Book*. It's just spellings of about 30,000 most used words. You'd be surprised how many words my program doesn't know. I also love my rhyming dictionary. But that's another story.

Okay, what is that "interesting stuff" you said you uncover online?

I check on the parole status of the murderers I have written about. Their getting out is unlikely, but I certainly want to know if they do. To find incarcerated persons, just use a search engine to find the Web site of the Department of Corrections in the state in question. In my case, it's the Illinois Department of Corrections [118]. The home page has an Inmate Search option. Click on that and you're there.

Do you have a Web site, and if so, how does it help your career as a writer? Do you think all writers should have their own site?

I don't have a Web site, but my son Rich Remsberg, the photographer, who just published his first book, *Riders for God: The Story of a Christian Motorcycle Gang*, has just put one up [222]. I'm watching his to see how it works out.

My friend and fellow writer Hal Higdon has a very successful site [112]. Hal is very good at making his books and services available. He sells and promotes through the Web. He has a targeted market, also, since much of his work is in the field of running, fitness, and health.

Do you subscribe to any electronic newsletters?

No newsletters. I try not to clutter up my electronic life too much. I try to keep the computer for writing, most of the time.

Are you in touch with other writers via the online medium?

I love the ASJA Forum. Informative, funny, like a good chat at the water cooler. And you can go whenever you want to. It's great solace and companionship. The ASJA forum is restricted to members—you can join ASJA at the web site [21]—and in my opinion is one of the principle benefits of membership. We talk about anything and everything, usually connected to writing but occasionally straying into life questions, always interesting ones. Much talk of rights, and clarification of that murky area. Research tips, Web tips, morale boosts—the whole enchilada.

Do you do any teaching online?

No. I have done a lot of teaching, but again, the old-fashioned way, in a room with the students. I like it that way.

What's your hardware setup and do you have a high-speed Internet connection?

Ordinary modem, ordinary computer. I am in no way high-tech. This is all I can manage and, at the moment, all I want. It still comes down to a blank sheet of paper, even when the paper is a screen, crying for you to fill it. A frightening prospect—exciting and rewarding, too.

Do you get published online?

Haven't gone for online publishing. I'm concentrating on plays now, and getting them produced in the real world is difficult enough without jumping into cyberspace. The theater is, by definition, an event involving real people in a room together. I like that, and need it.

If you had to think of only one way the Internet helps you as a writer, what would it be?

One of the best uses of the Internet for me is the ability to find and buy books. I particularly look for old ones that are hard or impossible to find elsewhere. Alibris [14], Bookfinders [39], Abebooks [9], Bibliofind [35], and so on have been helpful in turning up research books.

I have also ordered books from Amazon.com. I collect pop-up books and sometimes just can't resist something particularly yummy. I have also bought copies of my own books when they're really cheap at Half.com.

You are the type of writer who is not totally dependent on technology. What comments would you like to leave us with in regard to the Internet?

The Web has a tremendous upside, as we all agree. But the downside is just as tremendous, if not more so. Just as the car—convenient, liberating—changed society in so many ways, it also served to restructure our communities, to isolate us in myriad ways. The Web is doing, and will do, just as much.

I like going to the library. There are people there. I avoid ATMs and go into the bank. There are people there. We give up so much when we lose our sense of community. Pixel relationships are not face-to-face relationships, no matter how convenient. We need each other, and a screen is a screen. You can't hug it. It doesn't smile at you, or really know you. Most importantly, the screen doesn't care if you're there or not. My family does care. My friends do care. And I want my community to care too.

Super Searcher Power Tips

➤ I'm prone to migraines, and I almost automatically know that when I get into a Web site with flashing lights and stuff bouncing around, it's not only irrelevant, it's harmful.

➤ Since the advent of email, I find I can connect socially with people without that having to interfere with my work time. It is the most controllable socialization I can imagine.

➤ I love the ASJA Forum. Much talk of rights, and clarification of that murky area. Research tips, Web tips, morale boosts.

➤ One of the best uses of the Internet for me is the ability to find and buy books. I particularly look for old ones that are hard or impossible to find elsewhere. I have also bought copies of my own books when they're really cheap at Half.com.

➤ Writing still comes down to a blank sheet of paper, even when the paper is a screen crying for you to fill it.

Jodi Picoult
Reader-Friendly Novelist

Jodi Picoult, who at age thirty-four has eight novels and three children to her credit, was born and raised—happily—on Long Island. "I had such an uneventful childhood that, much later, when I was taking writing classes at college, I called home and yelled at my mother, wishing for a little incest or abuse on the side," recalls Picoult. "Good writers, I thought at the time, had to have something to write about. It took me a while to realize that I already did have something to write about—that solid core of family, and of relationships, which seem to form a connective thread through my books."

Her eight novels, which all center on what it means to love someone, have come out in rapid-fire succession: *Songs of the Humpback Whale* (1992), which Picoult wrote when she was six months pregnant with her first child; *Harvesting the Heart* (1994), which she describes as a reflection of her feelings as a new mother—and her most emotionally autobiographical novel; *Picture Perfect* (1995); *Mercy* (1996), a novel about married love and whether it's really 50/50 (Jodi says she and husband Tim are still debating this); *The Pact* (1998); *Keeping Faith* (1999); *Plain Truth* (2000); and *Salem Falls* (2001).

Jodi says she really learned to write at Princeton, where she studied creative writing with Mary Morris, who urged her to submit a story to *Seventeen* magazine. Picoult was stunned when they published it and a second story a bit later. "That's when I thought I could be a writer," she says.

However, when Jodi graduated from Princeton, she headed not for the word processor, but for Wall Street, and followed that with stints at a textbook publishing company and an ad agency. She also taught creative writing part-time at a high school, got her master's degree in education at Harvard, and married Tim, whom she'd known at Princeton. Soon she was pregnant and had written a thousand-page manuscript, which became *Songs of the Humpback Whale*.

It took a while, but Picoult says she has reconciled writing and motherhood. "I'm a better mother because I have my writing and I'm a better writer because of the experiences of motherhood that have shaped me." At this point, Picoult sees her list of novels growing, but not her family.

JpvanLeer@aol.com
www.jodipicoult.com

I know that you're just back from a book tour for your latest novel, *Salem Falls*. I just finished reading it and can see that you used the Internet for at least some of your research. Let me start with a general question, then I'll get to specifics. On the acknowledgments page *of Salem Falls*, your first line reads: "If I could cast a spell, like some of my protagonists in this novel, it would be one to acquire unlimited knowledge." Has the Internet been helpful to you in acquiring the knowledge needed to write fiction?

It is so hard for me to imagine, now, what life as a writer was like without the Internet. I use it extensively—to hop onto a search engine and find a quick answer to a question; to communicate with my experts, some of whom live in Australia; to do in-depth research before I start writing a book. It is like having a library at your fingertips at all times.

New York City is featured a bit in your book. In your acknowledgments page you thank someone for providing you with "a virtual tour of the Lower East Side." I'm assuming you took a digital tour via your computer screen.

Actually, that had nothing to do with computers! My ninety-year-old grandfather described in detail what life was like when he was growing up there.

One of your characters types in the word "Wiccan" and runs it through a search engine.

She comes up with 153,995 hits. Did that scene come from your own search?

Yes. When I was researching *Salem Falls,* I hung out on Wiccan Web sites, the teen message boards. Teens, it turns out, are the fastest growing group of Wiccans. One of the very nice things— and dangerous, too—about the Internet is that you can pretend to be someone else, and that can get you a lot of information, as it did in this case. I posted as a wannabe-teen-witch, and received lots of help and criticisms from mentor-witches, which put me in the right frame of mind to create my character, Gillian.

There's a lot of information about genes and DNA in the book as characters get ready for a trial. Was the Internet helpful with that? Do you ever search for scientific information on the Internet? If so, where?

Often, when I look up scientific information on the Internet, I either get very basic information that I already know, or I wind up in very specific Web sites geared to experts in various fields who have published papers on these topics. And most of the time, that's like reading Greek! The DNA information in the book came from a research contact of mine who does this for a living. She also referred me to some newspaper articles on preimplantation genetic diagnosis that I accessed online through Nexis. Those articles sparked not only the research for *Salem Falls,* but also for some of the subsequent novels I have been working on. They spiraled off into information about DNA and some of the newest procedures and techniques that are starting to run into the roadblock of medical ethics.

A teenage girl in your book types in "atropine," which is a drug, on a search engine and comes up with information about it. Did you try it—the

search, not the drug!—before you wrote about it? Do you look for medical information online, and if so, from which Web sites?

The sites that have been most beneficial to me when finding drug or medical info are drkoop.com [78, see Appendix], WebMD [267], and the ThriveOnline Health and Medical Section [248]. Sometimes I will type a drug name into a major search engine like Ask Jeeves [27] or Dogpile [76], and it will spit out a bizarre pharmaceutical site that offers up a wealth of information, like Drugtext [79]. And yes, I did try Gillian's search before I wrote it! In fact, her dosage levels for this drug came from Botanical.com [44].

There's a scene where a lawyer, in an effort to save an innocent man from years in prison, has to find someone's credit card number online. How did you learn the steps for doing that?

I was told by a private investigator that buying online has made tracing people extremely easy these days. She walked me through the steps, as outlined in *Salem Falls*. Basically, it involves hacking into someone's password file and then finding the electronic trail left behind on their computer's hard drive.

How big a part does email play in your career as a novelist?

I interview a lot of "research experts" via email. It's easier, since I can ask the questions on my own time, and I get a concrete record of the answers! I also receive a ton of email from fans. Since setting up my Web site in 1998, I receive between twenty and forty fan emails per day—and I answer every single one.

I love email. I think it's easier than writing a physical letter to an author you admire, and it also allows me to see, with great immediacy, the effect my books are having on my audience. Also, I send my chapters via email to my mother, my agent, my co-screenwriter, and a friend who is a novelist, and receive their critiques that way.

What about online forums—do you ever access them to talk with fellow writers?

I have never gone to an online writer's forum to speak with colleagues, but I have gone to many online chats with readers of my novels. I love doing that—it's like working in one's pajamas! At iVillage.com [130], there is a terrific author/reader chat series, as there is at Oprah.com [193]; check out her reading group stuff.

Do you subscribe to any electronic newsletters?

Unfortunately, I don't. Every time I try to, I wind up deleting them. I don't have time to read all the stuff I get!

You are one of those writers who has her own Web site. How has it helped you?

My Web site was launched in 1998 as a way to make my writing more accessible to readers, and to make me look more reader friendly. It was designed by James Taylor—not *that* James Taylor—a Webhead who lives near me. I love it because I think it's very easy to move around; not all readers are Internet savvy. It is updated annually with each new book that's published, and includes personal information about me, interviews, photos, reviews and discussion questions for my books, sample chapters, and even sneak peeks of what I'm working on. It also provides a direct link to my email address so people can write to me. This year, at the behest of my fans, I added a bulletin board so readers can talk to each other, as well as to me, about my books. The Web site has been a godsend. It makes people feel like they know me, I think, and it allows readers and reading groups to dig a little deeper into my books once they've read them.

Do you know any writers who are not using the Internet as you are? Do you have any advice for technophobes?

I know lots of writers who are not using the Internet. I think they're crazy! Yes, there is too much information out there, and sometimes a live person is better than a Web page. But there is also a great deal of information you can get as background before you hie off to do your research in person.

My best advice would be to start with a search engine like Ask Jeeves—it's so incredibly user friendly that you'll find yourself hooked.

What are your favorite search engines, and what do you do to make sure you don't get an overload of hits?

I love Dogpile because it accesses a multitude of engines at once. Sometimes I'll use Ask Jeeves, although I'm not always delighted with the hits. I refine my searches by clicking on a hit that looks "right" and then adding more keywords that might narrow down what I'm looking for.

What's your hardware setup, and do you have high-speed Net access yet? Have you been computer savvy long, or is it somewhat new with you?

I work on a Dell desktop and a Dell laptop with a big fat memory for all my novels; they're on the hard drive. I don't have high-speed access—hey, I live in New Hampshire! As for my computer savviness, I'm still a novice, and if you ask my techie brother he'll confess that he gets calls from me, hyperventilating, asking how to find the chapter that just blanked out from my screen.

Are you writing anything right now that you're using the Internet for?

The book I'm writing now is a ghost story. Not only did I use the Internet to find a bunch of real-live ghost hunters—whom I eventually met and went hunting with!—but I also stumbled upon a fabulous piece of Vermont history by doing searches on the Abenaki Indians—something that will play an important plot role. I am currently using a site [261] put together by Nancy Gallagher, a scholar who compiled a lot of documents that I'm using in excerpts for the novel. I also researched a very rare genetic skin condition called xeroderma pigmentosum, or XP, on the Internet for this same novel. I even used email to strike up a research relationship with a Rhode Island State Trooper, who eventually took me out on a Forensics 101 session to help me learn what I needed to for a particular character's job!

You've been wonderful, Jodi, in answering these questions right after a book tour, which I hear can be an exhausting experience. Do you mind, now, if I lift a few items of interest from your Web site concerning how you use the Internet?

Be my guest!

The following information is from novelist Jodi Picoult's Web site at www.jodipicoult.com.

What's the best part of your job?

The fans. Who wouldn't want to wake up to daily emails from people telling you how fantastic your writing is? Also, the fact that I do what I absolutely love to do. I don't think many people can say that about their jobs.

What about your writing makes you most proud?

The fact that I've literally worn the letters off two computer keyboards.

You're only thirty-four years old, and have written eight novels in nine years while bearing—and raising—three children. You must have an amazing writing regimen!

Regimen? No way. Does anyone with three kids under the age of ten have a regimen? I'm lucky to gather the scraps of my time and write when I can! Nothing I'm working on is as important as my children—which means that if one of them comes up to my office to show me a cut on his knee or to have me referee a war with her brother, that takes precedence. It has gotten easier since my husband became a stay-at-home dad this summer. I finally can go on tour without stressing over who will watch the kids; I can work straight through school pickup at 2:45 P.M. In making this life choice, my husband Tim has given me an incredible gift.

But for years I managed to squeeze in my writing where I could, and as a result of that, I've developed a discipline, if not a regimen. I am blessed with an ability to write very quickly, and I don't believe in writer's block, because I don't have time to believe it. I sit down and write, whether the stuff I type out is good or not, and edit later. Usually I thrash through a plot first, then characters, and finally a tentative ending (which, I discover, is usually not the way it ends at all ...).

I do my research, and then when I feel like I "know" enough to write, I work chapter by chapter. Whenever people look at my books, and then at my kids, and shake their heads and ask how I do it, I always want to ask back, "How couldn't I?" I wouldn't trade a moment with my children. And in return, my children know that I need to write like some people need asthma medication—

as a preventative, because when I don't write for a few days, I get predictably cranky.

How do you do your research?

Meticulously. I hate catching authors in inaccuracies when I'm reading, so I'm a stickler for research. At this point I have several folks "on call" for me during the writing of a book—a few lawyers, a few psychiatrists, some doctors, a pathologist, a DNA scientist.

When I begin to research a topic, I read anything I can about it. Then I immerse myself in the topic by meeting with an "expert." Some things are harder to find out about than others—getting the head of Launch Operations at NASA to squeeze me into his busy schedule, for example; or making a series of connections that landed me in the home of an Amish farmer for a week.

In the name of research, I've watched Sylvester Stallone on a movie set for *Picture Perfect*; I've gone to jail for the day for *The Pact*; I've observed cardiac surgery for *Harvesting the Heart*; I've milked cows on an Amish dairy farm for *Plain Truth*; I've learned DNA testing and Wiccan love spells for *Salem Falls*. I'm about to go ghost hunting with paranormal researchers for my next book.

How on earth did you get to research the Amish for *Plain Truth*?

Amazingly, through the Internet. After posting a query on a Lancaster County message board, I got a response from a lovely Mennonite woman, with whom I struck up a research relationship.

After many, many email queries, she suggested I come visit the area and volunteered to find me some Amish friends to stay with. I was there for a week, milking at 4:30 A.M. and participating in the morning Bible study, as well as helping out with the cooking of meals. I quickly learned that the Amish aren't the one-dimensional characters they're made out to be. Like us, there are good people and bad people, tolerant people and intolerant people, lenient people and more exacting people. Just because we grow up taught to live our lives differently doesn't necessarily mean our way is better.

Have you met many of your readers at book signings or through letters and email?

Yes! I love getting fan mail. The best part of this Web site has been the accessibility fans have to me via email. See that little mailbox on the top of the page? Please, email me and tell me what you thought of the book you read! The letters come right to me, and I always answer.

Often, when you're a writer, you don't know what your readers think of a book. You get feedback from critics and sales figures, but none of that is the same as knowing that you've made people stay up all night reading, or helped them have a good cry, or really touched their lives.

Recently I've been meeting book groups online to discuss my books, too. Sometimes people who have written to me or emailed me will come to a book signing, which is wonderful. Then I can put a face to the name. And every single time I get a letter or an invitation or meet a fan, I'm a little humbled and amazed. Deep down, I still sort of believe that the only people out there reading my books are relatives!

Super Searcher Power Tips

➤ For technophobes: My best advice would be to start with a search engine like Ask Jeeves—it's so incredibly user friendly that you'll find yourself hooked.

➤ I refine my searches by clicking on a hit that looks "right" and then adding more keywords that might narrow down what I'm looking for.

➤ Since setting up my Web site, I receive between twenty and forty fan emails per day—and I answer every single one.

➤ I have gone to many online chats with readers of my novels. I love doing that—it's like working in one's pajamas!

➤ I send my chapters via email to my mother, my agent, my co-screenwriter, and a friend who is a novelist, and receive their critiques that way.

➤ I know lots of writers who are not using the Internet. I think they're crazy!

Gary Gach
The Buddha Beat

Gary Gach was born in Los Angeles in 1947. He holds a B.A. in English (UCLA-SFSU) and held a number of day jobs before becoming a full-time writer, including book designer, bookstore clerk, encyclopedia salesman (one-half day), hospital administrator, legal secretary, magazine editor in chief, stevedore, temp, and web weaver, plus a stint as the next-to-last secretary of fantasy author Fritz Leiber, Jr. He's also acted on stage and screen and is a dynamic public speaker.

Gary is the author of the world's first mass market pocketbook guide to the Internet (*Pocket Guide to the Internet*, 1996), a communications medium that he says he co-developed with Al Gore. He followed that with *Writers.net: Every Writer's Essential Guide to Online Resources and Opportunities* (1997), which he intends to revise and have republished.

His anthology, *What Book!?—Buddha Poems from Beat to Hiphop*, was honored with an American Book Award in 1999. His latest book is *The Complete Idiot's Guide to Understanding Buddhism* (2001).

He's also completed a book about a changing China, so he seems to have a penchant for surveying big topics for the common reader. Upcoming projects include an illustrated haiku anthology/guide for younger readers; a book of poems entitled *All Ways*; and a series of short stories about a mortician. An as-yet unproduced screenplay is biding its time.

Translations in the works include a new rendition of Ecclesiastes and Proverbs, and an anthology, *Searching for Plum Blossoms in the Snow: 5,000 Years of Chinese Song* (with C. H. Kwock). Gary's own work has been translated into Arabic, Czech, Greek, and Korean.

His articles have appeared in *American Cinematographer*, *American Book Review*, *American Reporter*, *Christian Science Monitor*, *Information Age*, *Internet World*, *Multimedia Merchandiser*, *Multimedia Producer*, *Publishers Weekly*, *San Francisco Chronicle*, *San Francisco Examiner*, *San Francisco Review of Books*, *Shambhala Sun*, and *Yoga Journal*.

Gary has spent the majority of his life on Russian Hill in San Francisco.

gary@word.to
http://word.to

You write poetry and you write on topics in Eastern religion. Do you ever have the need to consult the Internet for those topics? Which Web sites have been helpful?

Each school of Buddhism has its own unique presence online. Access to Insight [7, see Appendix], for example, is a primary site for practitioners of vipassanna or insight meditation, a.k.a. Theravada Buddhism. One of my favorite top-level meta-portals in the whole buddhaverse is the WWW Virtual Library [275]. Their hyper-index of Buddhist studies resources [276] is impeccable.

For poetry, the Electronic Poetry Center at SUNY, Buffalo [83] does a brilliant job mapping the Net's potential for transforming poetry. They have links, for example, to a site devoted to things like animated poetry. The Electronic Poetry Center has pointed out that, just as the typewriter was formative in the development of modern poetry, so does the Net offer tools for new visions. For example, if a poem is no longer hard copy, when is it ever done? Fascinating.

For such a short form of literature as haiku, which is my big interest, there are quite a number of sites, many of them major. The Shiki Internet Haiku Salon [231], for example, is both a great portal and the site of a well-trafficked discussion group. A somewhat more specific haiku site might be Jane Reichold's Aha! Poetry site [132], the Web adjunct of Aha! Books. And to fill in the gaps, Alexey Andreyev's haiku page [13] is quite fine. Some of these overlap into related Eastern forms like tanka and sijo, and into poetry and publishing in general.

My favorite information sources, most days of the week, are threaded discussion groups, often with a home on the Web plus an option to participate by email as well. This is not to be confused with "chat," which is real time. For instance, Buddhist Peace Fellowship [46] has a sweet combination of news, events notices, and occasional impromptu discussion for folks around the world interested in engaged Buddhism—that is, Buddhism active in social and political issues. It doesn't have too many postings, so I can keep up without any heavy lifting, and, best of all, it does have a community of posters that have become very vivid to me, from all over the country and the globe. As with all email lists or online discussion groups, a main topic or thread can be the jumping-off point for various and sundry human affairs, branching off, looping the loop, and fanning out in all sorts of interesting byways.

For focused discussion, there are a couple dozen mailing lists devoted to Buddhism, such as Buddha-L [45]. Some Usenet groups discussing Buddhism include alt.zen, alt.religion. buddhism.tibetan, alt.religion.buddhism.theravada, and talk. religion.buddhism—whose FAQ file, or answers to Frequently Asked Questions, includes online scriptures, virtual communities, electronic journals, and other Net links—and the refreshingly and appropriately iconoclastic alt.buddha.short.fat. guy group. Overall, there seem to be more Buddhist sites than you can shake a sacred stick at.

As for poetry *and* Buddhism together, I'm happy to say that my own Web site, WhatWeb!? [269], does a pretty good job of sorting through the interrelationships.

Tell me about your interest in China.

I've written a book on China, unpublished. It's a picture of a country undergoing perhaps the fastest pace and largest scope of growth in human history. The background to my personal interest is a long story, including my co-translating Chinese poetry from all the dynasties with C. H. Kwock for ten years.

There's an interesting online angle. Many recall the explosion of information beginning in April 1989, when eyewitnesses from Tiananmen Square and elsewhere across China reported day-by-day, moment-by-moment turns of events. Coincidentally, North American China scholars had already formed a network about six months previously, *China News Digest* [53], the world's first Chinese magazine online. Besides providing daily news, it maintains a database on the Nanjing Massacre, the Cultural Revolution, classic literature, and so on.

You told me you're on deadline for an *Idiot's Guide*. What's it about and how are you using the Internet to write it?

I'm writing the series title on Buddhism for the Complete Idiot's Guide series, as we speak. Besides the stacks of books and magazines encircling my desk, plus my forays to libraries and Buddhist centers, the Internet's a great 24/7 resource with its own particular virtues and charms—especially given the tight turnaround this publisher favors.

If I can't remember a certain zen anecdote, for instance, I enter the few words or phrases I do remember into a search engine like Google [104] and find the full text, and maybe even different versions. It helps that Buddhism is a field whose adherents are posting a large body of doctrinal material online.

Email is, as always, indispensable: I've emailed chapters and sections to experts for a critique, which often results in ongoing email dialogue. Email is terrific for collaborative work in a short period of time across various time zones.

How else is the Internet featured in your day-to-day work as a writer?

As a general rule, passing files back and forth with editors is invariably done by email these days. It creates a text stream that's "fungible," rather than hard copy that would need to be retyped at the other end.

Right now I'm working on a short story cycle set at a funeral home, and doing a certain amount of Net research for background. I know that's intriguing, but I don't want to talk about it right now, since it's still in process.

I read an online interview with you where you say journalists should belong to at least two or three mailing lists, such as CARR-L, Computer-Assisted Reporting & Research [50]; JourNet, a journalism education list [136]; and IRE-L, Investigative Reporters and Editors [128]. Does this advice still stand and why?

Those plus SPJ-L, the Society of Professional Journalists list [236], are primary lists for journalists. Like all lists, they have their signal-to-noise ratios; that is, how often you find a gem amid all the hay. They tend to be very good during or after big events, sharing battle stories, for example. I'd also recommend a list for a regional writing group for more focused discussion as well as local news, plus lists pertinent to your beat.

I subscribe to Blue Ear Forum [38] for its international news perspective; RW-L, the Romance Writers' List [225], for nuts-and-bolts about backstory, dialogue, characterization, and so on; Online Writing list, which is also associated with a Webzine for online writers, Contentious [63]; plus I frequent some of the writing, media, and books forums at The WELL [247].

To subscribe to a mailing list, you often have to send email with a "subscribe" request to an automated list manager. That's the routine drill for email-based lists. This is followed by your receiving a welcome notice with instructions that you should save in a separate file somewhere, in case you ever decide to unsubscribe. You may also have to email back a confirmation in order to be put on the list initially. You may also have the option of subscribing in digest mode, which means getting all the day's email in one lump, with a table of contents, and the ability to search the list archives for topics that have been discussed in the past. For optimal management of lists, I recommend setting up your email reader to filter all email from each list into its own file folder.

Which search engines do you use and why?

Recently I was surprised when talking with someone who works for a big search engine company and hearing him say he uses Google rather than the one he works for. It's the search engine of choice right now, usually turning up the right answer in a streamlined fashion. Its acquisition of Deja, which allows you to search Usenet postings, and its ability to search PDF (Adobe's Portable Document Format) files rack up extra points in its favor. Check out the advanced features; if nothing else, put phrases within quotes to narrow the search parameters.

What else? I like About.com [3], which uses a human expert as gatekeeper or aggregator of information, subject by subject.

Multisearch engines are an excellent way to get a sense of what's out there in terms of both information and the sites providing coverage. The latest one I've been using has been Dogpile [76]. Meanwhile, I'm anticipating 3-D search engines. Thirty years from now I'll look at what's available and wonder what if it were all available to me as I am today, and shudder. The Net is developing at an exponential rate. What if people who called their car a "horseless carriage" could have had any idea of what a jet plane is? Now imagine what if people just beginning to use a wax tablet and a stylus for writing could envision the Internet.

You mentioned a Web site of yours that you casually call Research Central [219]. Could you tell us about it?

When I wrote my book, *Writers.net*, I wanted a Web adjunct to do two things: to provide more up-to-date information on new developments and sites as well as info on changed links, and to create something of value to give back to the Net, being of the opinion that the Net is a commons. So I created an all-in-one search portal. Back in 1997, "portal" wasn't a common word yet; I called them "megasource jumpstations."

From my arrangement and annotation of the links, you can still glean some useful tips, such as differentiating between searching broad and narrow. Many of the links themselves are still good, too; others have been superseded or disappeared. A visit to the home page for the updates [220] reflects the outline of the book; many of the links are still good. I haven't tended my home pages for over a year, but plan to do yard work this summer—weeding, grafting, adding new cuttings, as well as posting a Web adjunct to my next book.

What role does email play in your working life?

While the Web's gotten all the publicity, it's email, along with various kinds of discussion groups, that's the lifeblood of the Net for me: people communicating. If time-and-motion experts were to break down my online habits, they'd probably find I spend ninety percent of my online time communicating and ten percent or less on the Web.

Email has its own distinct advantages. Sometimes it's easier to get past gatekeepers—at the doors of, say, publishing firms—by using email instead of voice mail. Email is less in-your-face than the phone, allows the other party to reply at their leisure, along with optional amenities like quoting what they're replying to, including attachments, sending copies and blind copies to other recipients, and so on.

An example: I was casting out a net for sources once and was passed along to a very difficult person to reach via someone who acted as a go-between judiciously writing the source a letter, with a cc: to me, inviting both of us to contact each other directly. That would be less likely to happen face-to-face, or by cold-calling on the phone. It might have been possible via hard copy letters, but with more friction to the third party in terms of making separate copies and envelopes.

I use email for all phases of my work: for research; for correspondence with agents, publishers, editors, and publicists; and for getting a closer sense of my audience before or after publication. If you include your email address you're more likely to get letters than if you include your post-office box.

Have you ever used ProfNet [202] or similar services to gain access to experts or press releases?

ProfNet has consistently furnished me with access to sources, who generally want attribution. A great many, if not the majority, of ProfNet sources come through Public Information Officers, so it's essentially flak. Expect spin. For business sources, Business Wire [48] has about 8,500 sources on tap, though that's not necessarily the best avenue if you're only fact-checking. There's a lesser known site out there called SourceNet [234], but I haven't tried it.

One online resource nonfiction writers, particularly journalists, can turn to for disinterested third-party experts is FacsNet [90], maintained by the Foundation for American Communications, a nonprofit that provides what I'd call headspace for journalists. The site includes a database of sources, with bios, so you can know about their background and pick whom you want to talk to. Also, they're screened by journalists; nobody's paying a PR firm for a listing. You don't have to be a journalist for access, but they do ask for registration. You'll get announcements of upcoming symposia, and they won't sell the list. In the interests of full disclosure, I was a research fellow there last year. I created the only Web site on the Net at FacsNet for journalists to cover Y2K.

You have a Web site. Do you think all writers should have their own? How has yours helped your career as a writer?

I've had a Web site for about four years. I'd say it's a good hobby, if you have the time. I'll give you an example of how it's also useful. The local daily fishwrap hired a new book editor, and I wanted to introduce myself and see if he'd assign me to review a certain book. So I called him up, congratulated him, introduced myself and my pitch, and said that if he wanted writing samples, I have a Web site, or I could mail him some clips. He asked me the URL. Then, in the blink of an eye, he was thumbing through my portfolio as we spoke. It was fun, and saved me the awkwardness of saying, "Yes, I mailed you clips on Friday the 13th," and waiting while the party at the other end sorts through piles of papers on the floor.

Relative to book publishing, the Web has its advantages, too. Book publication can be like heaving a huge boulder over a cliff. You stand there and wait, but you might never know what happens afterwards, if anything. A guest book is a great tool on a personal Web site. It lets you get a better sense of who might be out there and what they might think of your work.

I have no idea about personal Web sites and online book sales. The sizzle of online book sales has leveled off in general. But as you're competing with at least 50,000 other titles in this year's pipeline, it helps, I think, to generate some attention for your own ink-smeared, dead-tree edition—that the trees should not have gone on in vain.

I also like the expandability of the Web as a means of providing an adjunct to a book. Actually, the Web adjunct to my Buddhist poetry anthology [269] now has more material than the bookstore version, so I wonder which is the adjunct of which?

I've read where you likened the Internet/ computer revolution to the Gold Rush—the people who made the money were the people who sold tools to the prospectors. You also likened the Internet/computer revolution to "the saloon keepers who waited for a railroad to come through town. The railroads *will* come through, and *are*." In view of the fact that the Internet revolution is coming, do you envision the day when writers will find everything they need in regard to research on the computer?

Gawd, I hope not! That would be as extreme as the opposite idea of the entire Net becoming a ghost town. Draw a circle and see how many things you can find inside it: then step outside that circle and look some more. Even if it's a magic circle. Diversity rules. Expand your horizons.

By the way, speaking of the computers taking over, have you heard: some sports writers have been laid off, lately, replaced by a software program that can generate copy from online information? Is that an urban legend among writers? I've seen it sourced to the *Wall Street Journal,* but I haven't gotten a second source yet. And in Hollywood, there's the tale of the writers who run out of inspiration and input a few story synopses from *TV Guide* program listings into some software package and come up with new ideas for their show.

Since I've made you aghast at my hypothetical picture of an Internet-only research world, now's a good time to ask: How often do you turn to noncomputer sources, like the library, print books—including your own—and so on?

Using my own books doesn't always apply since I tend to write about different things each time; I don't want to repeat myself. Maybe if I start deciding on a regular beat. Sometimes I do go back to recycle quotes, for epigrams and such-like, in new contexts.

In general, it's amazing the synchronicity that happens when you become immersed in a topic: You can overhear a conversation in an elevator and know exactly how it would fit into your text: Chapter Three, after the third paragraph. When I'm doing research, I listen to the intelligent voices on the radio and talk to perfect strangers on the bus. I've talked to friends. I've hung out at lunch tables where sources I'm looking for tend to eat.

I'm on a first-name basis with a number of indispensable research librarians, and occasionally reach out to new ones. For example, did you know the Reference Desk at the New York Public Library [178] takes long-distance phone calls?

Do you use online or CD-ROM reference resources—dictionary, thesaurus, encyclopedia, quotation books? Have any favorites?

I use the *Encyclopaedia Britannica* CD-ROM, but I hear that's online now.

Do you subscribe to any paid subscription services like Dialog or LexisNexis?

Technically, no. But now that The WELL has dropped Usenet, I'll probably be paying a Web site like NewsGuy [175] to subscribe to newsgroups.

Do you ever look up graphics online?

I haven't really gotten my feet wet yet. I've looked at usual suspects like Photonica [199] and Corbis Stock Market [66] for inexpensive shots. I found Ditto.com [75] for some basic images, through About.com Web Search's relatively small collection of image finders.

I did look at two photographers' portfolios on the Web for plates for my current book. I found the photographers either by doing a search for their name, or by visiting the Web site of their company as listed in a photo credit for a shot I'd seen that caught my eye. Another photo I'm using I acquired by conducting a people search for the name of an author who happened to have shot a photo I could use, and he emailed it to me as an attachment.

Where do you go on the Internet to find newspaper or magazine articles?

Lately, I like Moreover [168] and HeadlineSpot [113]. I turn to specific news sources for specific topics, like *Ha'aretz* online edition [109] for news from Israel.

What sources do you turn to—online or print— to keep up with news about Web sites and computer advances?

Net-happenings [174]. Internet Scout [125]. The Monday and Thursday *New York Times*—Monday for the business section, and Thursday for "Circuits," the technology section. I liked *TechWeek,* from Silicon Valley, but it seems to have gone dark. *Syllabus* magazine [241], which is about distance learning, keeps me abreast of basic tech trends.

What's your hardware setup, and do you have a high-speed connection yet?

I'm typing away on a Mac 5400/120. I have a 56K modem, until I decide on my high-speed connection. I've added extra memory and have a 100 MB Zip disk attachment. Plus I've added auxiliary speakers since I'm fond of Internet radio, RealAudio interviews, and Webcasts, and I also use my computer to play CDs while I work.

On a related note, for more than a decade I've remained true to The WELL, the Whole Earth 'Lectronic Link, which Katie Hafner recently spotlighted in a book [287]. The Institute for Global Communications [121] deserves a V-sign too, in my opinion. Like Indian trails that follow vital paths of rivers or mountains, IGC and The WELL have been trailblazers in fostering and maintaining virtual communities, online circles of mutual interest. Both are online services that provide opportunities for creative interaction among their members. Each has a different focus. IGC plays a seminal role in assisting economically underdeveloped countries cross the Internet threshold through their sister organization, Association for Progressive Communicators [30], and maintains timely databases for activists in environmental affairs, social work, gender and racial equality, and global peace. In addition to discussion groups in those areas, they provide action alerts, alternative news feeds, event calendars, and other timely information.

The WELL is a more general community, focused more on occasions for users to interact. The users create the content. As Katie documents in her book, members have greeted their peers' first children online, and held online memorials to those passing out of life. I think of the story that early WELL-ite Howard Rheingold relates about the time his daughter came home with a huge tick on her shoulder. While his wife phoned 911, Howard went online and asked a forum at The WELL what to do, came back with a detailed concise plan of treatment, and followed through with it before the ambulance arrived.

I really enjoy interacting with brain scientists and cyberpunks, readers and authors, avatars and amateurs. But then, I'm curious about all branches of the human experience—the continually unfolding story of human possibility.

I know I'm digressing here, but do you really listen to CDs while you are writing?

If plants grow better under the influence of Mozart, why shouldn't our own work be affected by the ambient sounds in our environment!? But I do tend to turn the volume down to almost subaudible. That is, I turn it down to inaudible, then back up just a hair, then fine tune that a little until it's in some kind of precise comfort zone that only I know. Listening to the radio while working, of course, I hear the ads and the announcers' patter as part of the programming. So I tend to listen to a classical channel; the programming is fairly innocuous.

When you travel to China, do you stay connected via laptop and modem so you can check email and Web sites?

Since my primary email account is at The WELL, it's accessible via telnet. So wherever I travel, I jump onto a computer with a Web connection and telnet in to check my mail. In China, this could be at a university library, if not a friend's house or even an Internet cafe.

Telnet was the original application of the Internet, enabling users to access to remote computers. Telnetting into an ISP that supports that function, you enter your ID and password, and you're in. It's also very good for surfing library catalogues. I found some great information about China from a library in the Philippines, for example.

How and why did you get so computer savvy?

I think I'm pretty much a technopeasant, actually. My Aunt Muriel's far more advanced than me. After using a Tandy laptop as training wheels, I used a Mac and found it fairly intuitive.

Plus I'd been typing since elementary school. My father brought home a recycled IBM "B"-model for me to play with. I took typing instead of shop—except for print shop, where I hand-set some William Blake. As a day job, I worked temp in many offices with my skills as a typist and a wordsmith, and learned more word-processing programs than I care to think about.

What general advice do you have for writers with regard to conducting the best searches— that is, finding the pertinent information and avoiding the inaccurate information.

One rule of thumb is to gauge information in relation to its context. A chat room might have anybody yakking about anything; a subscription-only list like WriterL@telix.com [273] or a private, by-invitation-only list or discussion group can be high-energy peer learning at its best.

So check your source. Bore deeper into who's behind a site, and why they are posting it. Look at domain names, for example. A dot-com usually has some kind of sponsorship: How much do the sponsors shape content? Remember the journalist's golden rule: "He who owns the gold, rules." A dot-org can have its own bias, but it's usually more overt about it. Theoretically, a dot-edu should be a disinterested third party. We'll see if and how all this changes when new domain names take effect, like dot-info.

Another basic ethic of journalism applies for avoiding inaccurate information: "Source and double source." In other words, know your source but also get a second opinion. Some people tend to think anything's true if it's up on the Internet, the way people used to say, "It must be true, it's right there in black and white in today's newspaper."

Stay up to date. Librarians and other professional researchers offer tutorials that can make good reality checks every other year or so. Even if you only learn one new application or resource, it can be well worth it.

As a noted expert on the Internet and its effect on writing, what do you have to say about how the Internet has changed how writers do their research—which is, after all, the foundation of most writing?

Hey, flattery will get you everywhere. Actually, I'm just a relatively early adopter who had the good fortune to survey the field during its formative sweet spot. Internet experts there may be, but I ain't one of them.

Anyway, the Internet can erase boundaries of time and space. For nonfiction, background, statistics, human interest quotes— all the material for a whole feature—can be pulled in from the Net. For fiction, ditto for background; it's also a safe space for discussing elements of craft as well as researching atmosphere.

The Net's also a good way to research markets for writers— who takes unsolicited work, which agencies are bogus.

I wonder about your suggestion that research is *the* foundation of all writing. I agree it's foundational. But organization of material counts too. In nonfiction, it's often called spin. In fiction, it's called craft. Either way, research may turn up facts, but putting them *in formation* is equally as important. Storytelling, y'know.

What do you say to writers who are still tentative about the whole computer and Internet thing? In other words, they're technophobic and resisting?

Depends on the person. To some people, I smile and quote the joke Marshall McLuhan liked: "Didja hear what one caterpillar said to the other caterpillar when the butterfly floated by? 'You'll never get *me* up in one of those things!'" To others, I'd say, "Ignorance is bliss! Enjoy it while you can!" Lord Dunsany wrote everything with a quill pen, you know, and his work reads that way. Different strokes. But for those who'd like to be enticed, I just appeal to their instinctual curiosity. After all, isn't that at the root of writing?

Is there any advice you'd like to leave us with?

I'll give you my list:

1. Fit the Internet into the ecology of your communication. Ecology looks at the interrelationship of parts to create a whole. Previously, the ecology was phone-letter-and-lunch. Yesterday, I hung up the phone, faxed something, and then they called me back. This morning, my editor and I discussed something over the phone that would've taken several emails back and forth to hash out, and resolved a major thorny issue in five or ten minutes. Other times, email can be better. This applies, too, for Web sites, threaded discussion groups, and so on.

2. Keep track of the time. Computers are chroniverous: They eat time. You know what I mean if you've ever sat down at the computer just after sunset, then looked at the clock and wondered how it suddenly got to be so late, so fast. My own philosophy here is the jewel thieves' motto—the three Gs: Get in, get the money, get out. Thus, I use Lynx, a text-only browser, for most of my Web surfing, so I'm not slowed down by graphics I don't need

to see. It's my low-bandwidth, by-your-bootstraps form of high-speed access.

3. Watch out for the carpal at the end of the tunnel. Don't put your hands down and reach up to type, or hang your hands over the keys so your fingers have to drop down. Keep your wrists bent back instead of forwards. Also, try a mousepad with a wrist rest. Check out the appropriate distance and height for your keyboard. Stretch for five minutes every hour. And check out your posture— shoulders back, your lower back curved in, and so on.

Let me mention a few more Web sites we haven't touched on that may be useful: Itools [129] gives you access to reference tools including specialized dictionaries for computing, rhyming, pronunciation, and legal terms; biographical dictionaries; translators in more than twenty-five languages; and *Bartlett's Quotations*. Refdesk [217] is another comprehensive reference portal. Onelook [189] is a portal to dictionary sites in all languages on the Web; you enter a word and have your pick of dictionaries that contain a definition. Along the same lines, there's Online Dictionary Net [192] and Joe deRouen's page [134], which also includes encyclopedias, quote books, and other reference sources. For quotes specifically, try Jindagi's Wordsmith site [133], and the aptly named Find a Quotation [97], which calls itself the only portal on the Internet for quotations and sayings.

For investigative journalism, I like Padraic Cassidy's Web Page [195], which features a slew of handouts, many of which he's gathered over the years at panels of the annual convention of Investigative Reporters and Editors. To track plagiarism on the Web, you can try Findsame.com [99]. And for overall research purposes, ZDNet's SearchIQ [230] portal offers a good assortment of general and specialized search engines, subject databases, and collections of links.

Super Searcher Power Tips

➤ The Electronic Poetry Center has pointed out that, just as the typewriter was formative in the development of modern poetry, so does the Net offer tools for new visions.

➤ If I can't remember a certain zen anecdote, I enter the few words or phrases I do remember into a search engine like Google and find the full text, and maybe even different versions.

➤ While the Web's gotten all the publicity, email and various kinds of discussion groups are the lifeblood of the Net for me.

➤ Professional mailing lists are primary resources for journalists. They tend to be very good during or after big events, sharing battle stories, for example.

➤ For nonfiction especially, background, statistics, human interest quotes—all the material for a whole feature—can be pulled in from the Net.

➤ I like the expandability of the Web as a means of providing an adjunct to a book.

Paula Berinstein

Super at Searching

Paula Berinstein's first book was *Communicating with Library Users*, an endeavor that grew out of her work as a researcher and reference librarian. She published two others along that line: *Finding Images Online* [285, see Appendix] and *Finding Statistics Online* [286]. Gradually she began to branch out, writing books that were farther and farther afield from her career—books about technology, and energy, and space, the last a passion that brought her together with her English husband.

As far as research goes, she attributes her mania for digging to her grandmother's habit of "looking it up," which rubbed off on her. "We were a curious family," she says, winking at the double entendre—always wondering what, what if, how, why.

As a reference librarian, she gleefully rooted around in books and online services to answer other people's questions. Then she segued into information technology, where she constructed systems that allowed people to answer questions for themselves. Finally, she founded her own company, Berinstein Research, and once again turned to answering questions from others.

Paula writes articles about science and technology, information and communication, and business. From 1997 to 1999, she wrote a regular column in *Online* magazine called *The Big Picture*, which offered tips on finding images and explored the issues surrounding their use. She's proudest of "Moving Multimedia: The Information Value in Images," published in *Searcher* in September 1997, in which she proposed a simple way to classify images according to their purpose.

Paula has about five novels in her head: an astronomy thriller, a comedy set in a library, a historical piece that takes place in the Far East, a Tom Hanks/Meg Ryan-type story involving laundry, and one other that she's forgotten but is in her Palm Pilot. But who knows? A better idea could come along anytime.

paulab@berinsteinresearch.com
www.berinsteinresearch.com

Let's start with email. How does it figure in your researching for the books and articles you write?

Hugely! I often contact potential interviewees by email, though I phone too, often after I've initiated contact by email. I also subscribe to a variety of relevant email discussion and/or broadcast lists that I find—usually at the beginning of a project. Writing a book without email would take years longer. It's so hard to get in touch with people otherwise. And it's very convenient when you and the interviewee have different schedules. One of my interviewees right now lives in Japan. Not only would it be expensive to call him, but the time difference is something of a barrier, though not as much as it is for people I contact in the U.K.

Let me say a little more about these email discussion and broadcast lists. They are lifesavers. You can glean information without having to address a specific person. And you can follow the news. For example, for my book on alternative energy, I subscribed to a variety of lists that post developments in solar, wind, and biomass energy, fuel cells, alternative vehicles, and the like.

While I sought information from other sources as well, the news I got from these lists was often unique and added value to the book. One great thing about the email discussion lists is that you can identify people you might want to interview from the postings. It doesn't take long to identify an outstanding contributor, and they're easy to contact because—*voilà*—you have their email address right there. Of course, they don't always respond, but that's rare. You can be ignored and/or rebuffed in email the same as you can be by phone or in person. When I figure out how to prevent that from happening, I'll let you know.

The other thing you can do with email is gain permission to use tables and images. You just dash off a little text to the permissions department or Webmaster or whoever, and usually you get an answer back. Okay, I have to admit that sometimes it isn't a very prompt answer, and sometimes they demand ridiculous terms, but at least it doesn't cost anything to try.

How would writers go about finding email discussion lists for the topics they are interested in?

There are Web sites that provide lists of them. Try these two on for size: Liszt [148] and List of Lists [147]. By the way, you can find these two and a fabulous array of other search tools, like almanac and dictionary searches, and people search tools, and publication lists, at the All-in-One Search Page [15]. I highly recommend this site as a research starting point.

What computer system do you use?

I have a 500 MHz Sony VAIO laptop with Windows 98. I'm dying for a lighter-weight laptop because I travel so much. You put this leaden thing in a carry-on, and on some transatlantic flights they won't let you bring it into the cabin!

Do you use any software to organize the data you retrieve from the Web? What email software do you use?

As far as data I've retrieved is concerned, I just put that into Win 98 folders. Sometimes I print hard copies and file them in manila folders, though a lot of the time I stick hard copies in piles placed in strategic locations around my office—read "the floor." I use Eudora for email, again sorting messages into folders that are organized by topic. I also take advantage of Eudora's search facility to find messages I vaguely remember but can't find. I'm really very bare-bones about the way I organize things. I don't have the time to try all this fancy new software. I'm too busy writing!

Do you have high-speed Internet access yet?

Don't get me started! I've been trying to get a fast Internet connection for a year, and I still don't have one. First it was DSL. Well, as everyone knows by now, the whole industry has flaked.

Eeek—can I be sued for saying that? Part of the reason was that my husband and I live in the boonies, and they don't provide service here yet, but there was also, shall we say, a substantial lack of interest on the part of the companies we contacted. Now it's satellite, which has been promised and promised. They say they'll know something in a couple of days, but I've heard that for the last month. So I'm still humming along on 56K, if that.

Do you use online encyclopedias and dictionaries?

Once in a while. The online encyclopedias don't usually have the depth I'm looking for. Dictionaries are good for building glossaries, though. Or if you can't figure out what some abbreviation or acronym means.

You can find both general and specialized—science, medical—dictionaries at Refdesk.com [217], and lots of specialized dictionaries, such as those dealing with art, aerodynamics, and military terms at my very favorite reference meta-site, Martindale's The Reference Desk [157].

Do you ever go to the library to do research?

Yes. When I was writing my statistical handbook on technology, I went to the library to browse through the trade magazines in various fields so that I could find both data and leads on where to get them. I went mostly to the UCLA Engineering Library, where I interned when I was in library school. It was fantastically useful.

You just can't get a lot of that information online. Back issues may or may not be available, and sometimes you have to be a subscriber just to look. When you browse through the printed copy, you can usually spot tables immediately, whereas finding statistics in an online copy of a trade journal is a lot more hit and miss. As you know from my book, *Finding Statistics Online,* a lot of times the really important tables are omitted from the online versions. Grrrr.

Regarding the writing of *Statistics*, do you remember where you first looked online?

I always take a multipronged approach when I start research- ing a new book, so I initiate a lot of searches simultaneously. The first couple of things I did with this one weren't actually online. I started with Leonard Fuld's book *Competitor Intelligence: How to Get It, How to Use It* [284]. Here I began to identify some good sources of statistics, like trade magazines.

I then went to the UCLA Management Library and whatever they're calling the government documents library these days and looked at *American Statistics Index,* another large statistics index whose name escapes me at the moment, and some of the busi- ness indexes.

Then I looked at statistical compilations like almanacs, the *Statistical Abstract of the U.S.,* and similar volumes to see what I could get and who I could get it from.

Then I started looking up a lot of these sources online, also checking out the various government web sites like the U.S. Census Bureau [254], the Federal Communications Commission [96], et cetera. I also did a Dialog [72] search using various key- words to find articles that included the kinds of statistics I wanted. This got me the actual data, and it helped me identify sources. Then I just started following links and looking up organ- izations that were named on Web sites or in articles, and I was off.

What are your favorite search engines and favorite search tips?

I always start with AltaVista [16] because it seems to me that it offers the broadest coverage of the Web. But a lot of times it brings up too many false hits, so I go with others. Northern Light [185] is an excellent one because it searches not just the Web, but special document collections, too. It also seems to come up with more items of relevance than AltaVista does, but, as I say, its coverage isn't as broad. Sometimes I use HotBot [115] too, because it often brings up relevant items, though far fewer than the other two I've mentioned. Yahoo! [277] is also a favorite, especially when I need to identify companies. As for tips for searching them, well, I almost always use phrase searching rather than a jumble of terms higgledy-piggledy. Phrase searching narrows the search. Another tool I use is the "title:" feature on AltaVista, which limits the search to page titles—another good way of narrowing. Looking at the results list can usually suggest alternate terms; that's just standard search technique, isn't it? That's really it in a nutshell.

You are the only author in this book who is a professional searcher. Does that imbue you with more confidence than other writers, and do you feel it gives you an edge when it comes to research-heavy writing projects?

Oh yes, I have a lot of confidence in my research ability. After more than twenty years, I'd have to! I'd say I bring a lot of different kinds of helpful knowledge to my book research. For one thing, I know a lot of the sources, so I don't have to flail around as much as some people would. I also know how to formulate searches—select keywords, use proximity, and other features that help narrow down the material to that which is most relevant. I know how to follow trails, a hugely important skill in doing research, and how to mix it up by using a variety of approaches. For example, I use the telephone liberally. You have to. There's so much you either can't get any other way or that it would take you forever to get using other approaches. I don't mind going to the library—planting myself there if necessary. I love libraries, though the dust makes me sneeze. I'm even sort of writing a novel that takes place in a library. There's this Egyptologist, who's become a street person, and...

The publisher of your book *Finding Images Online* tells me that you offered to do the book first, and then figured out how to find images online second. Do you like the challenge of researching a totally new subject?

Yes, that's how I did it. I seem to have a penchant for choosing subjects about which I know almost nothing. I love the challenge! Aside: About ten years ago, I decided that I was becoming a fuddy-duddy, that I was really out of it and not keeping up. Boy, did I change!

The searching I did for *Finding Images Online* involved using not just the Web, but a variety of other online systems as well: America Online, CompuServe, GEnie, Kodak Picture Exchange, and others. Some of those no longer exist, or have become less popular. The Web wasn't all that far along at the time. Most people were still using Gopher [105] and Usenet [259] for posting and trading pictures. So it was a real challenge to learn and evaluate each separate system.

Now it's easier because it's mostly just the Web. Back then there were a gazillion search engines, and I took them all so seriously. Now I use only a small portion of what's available, as I mentioned in my response to your search engine question. I've become a lot more focused in how I search the Web now. I don't generally throw a lot of keywords at a search engine and let them fall where they may. On the other hand, the Web is slightly more organized and standardized now, and I understand much more about the content providers than I did. They're mostly established businesses, many of which were already in existence before the Web became popular, which they weren't at the beginning.

The book you are writing now is called *Making Space Happen*, and it's about the private efforts to establish a permanent human presence in

space. Have you interviewed many of the experts via email?

No. The only one I interviewed almost completely by email is the fellow in Japan I mentioned before. In at least one other case, I've sent follow-up questions by email. Mostly I've done in-person interviews, with some by telephone. And if you don't think it takes some doing to get to all these people…. Fortunately I've been able to catch up with some of them at conferences. In fact, I found out about most of them at conferences in the first place.

You also wrote *Alternative Energy: Facts, Statistics, and Issues*, which is a reference book about energy. You say the research was massive. Between this book and the space one, you have been dealing with a lot of science information. Are there any Web sites you would recommend for science information?

Science magazine [227], which is published by the American Association for the Advancement of Science, is a good one. They offer an online subscription and search facility. *Scientific American* [228] is another excellent source. Depending on what you're looking for, the National Science Foundation [173] may be helpful, though mostly they gather statistics about science rather than offering substantive information. Jim Martindale's great metasite, which I mentioned earlier, includes tons of links to science references. I've used his site a lot, and while I'm at it, I'd like to thank him for the great resource.

Of course, Medline [161] is always helpful for medical-related information. Infotrieve offers free access to Medline on its site. The U.S. Department of Energy, in particular the Energy Information Administration [255], was a big help, both online and on the phone, in the research for the energy book. I must have been responsible for about 30 percent of their hits during 1999 and 2000.

I also found various associations and advocacy groups extremely helpful for the energy book—sources like the Union of Concerned Scientists [253], the Worldwatch Institute [272], American Wind Energy Association [22], and various other environmental organizations. Even the Environmental Protection Agency [86] was somewhat helpful, though their Web site is a nightmare to use.

Of course, basic literature searches are extremely helpful. I use Dow Jones Interactive [77] extensively, especially their Publications Library, plus Northern Light. I also used NewsPage [176] for current awareness. BioMedNet [37], which provides medical and other life science articles, is another good one.

I can't say enough good things about trade magazines as sources, too. But there are tons of others, many of them subject-specific, such as Hollywood Reporter [114] and Space News [235]. I could go on forever. The other thing is the WWW Virtual Library [275], which is always a good starting place because it's a collection of metasites organized by subject. You can find guides to everything from chemistry to law to history there.

How accurate is the information you're finding on the Web?

Good question. I don't trust information from personal sites. As far as accuracy is concerned, I believe there is no such thing. Everyone is biased or uses different methodology. Sometimes you can get confirmation by finding the same information from multiple sources, but usually they all say different things, so it's very difficult. Call an expert and you have the same problem.

Where do you go to find newspaper articles online? In which instances would you need to refer to them?

Dow Jones Interactive is my favorite source for those. Sometimes I go to the Web site of particular publications, but you can go crazy trying to find something because their search features are often inadequate. Worse, even before you get that far, they present you with a number of obstacles, like registering and getting a password. Not only do you waste time with all this folderol, but you also have to keep track of umpteen user IDs and passwords. I use magazines and newspapers for pretty much all my work. A lot of them are good for overview articles on a topic, and they're very valuable for leads to other sources.

Speaking of Dow Jones Interactive, is it a subscription service these days or can anyone access it free of charge? If it is a subscription, do you subscribe, and how much does it cost?

There are several ways you can do it. I did it once the smart way and once the stupid way. The smart way is to register free for Qpass [208], an online payment system that lets you use a variety of sites like DJ Interactive, the *LA Times* [150], and so on. You don't pay anything to register; you only pay for the content. You can sign up for a plan that gives you twenty articles a month for $25. Or you can pay Dow Jones' per-article price of about $2.95. The stupid way, in my opinion, is to pay $69 per year through Dow Jones/Factiva and then pay by the article. The only good thing about that is that you get your first ten articles for free.

Speaking of paid subscription services, do you access Dialog, which goes back before the days of the Web and which professional searchers depended on?

I haven't used Dialog in ages. Truth is, it's kind of expensive for writers. The pricing structure is very complicated because each database charges differently. You're also billed for online time. There *is* a transactional service where you can pay by credit card on a per-article basis. Costs seem to run between about $3.50 and $4.50 per. It's hard to say exactly what each search is going to cost you on Dialog, but I can tell you that the cost will be more than on Dow Jones. For example, a full-text view of the *Atlanta Journal and Constitution* is $2.60. One DialUnit is $1.00. Don't even ask me about DialUnits. It's an artificial construct Dialog came up with for charging for clock time. So, at a minimum, one article is $3.60. Other databases are more expensive.

Now, I have to say that Dialog has just about the best content you'll find anywhere. The array of databases is staggering. They're definitely de rigeur for a lot of searches. But if the source is available at Dow Jones, I'd definitely go there rather than Dialog.

Some writers don't feel comfortable with computers or online searching. Do you have any advice to ease them into the technology?

Sit with me and I'll help you. Seriously, I don't know of a painless way to get started other than by sitting with someone who knows what they're doing and is a good explainer.

Do you have a Web site of your own? And do you think it's beneficial for writers to have one?

Yes. It's my Berinstein Research site [34]. This site promotes my research business rather than my writing business, but in the past I've used it to showcase my books.

I definitely think writers should have their own Web sites. There's so much published and so much noise about books and other products that you have to make a bit of your own noise to get the word out. Unless you're Stephen King or someone like that, it's going to be tough, so, yes, do as much publicity as you can, and build up your brand.

Do you have a general search tip you'd like to leave us with?

Use phrase searching as much as possible to keep results on target. And here's another one: Get a toehold and follow trails.

Super Searcher Power Tips

➤ Dow Jones Interactive is my favorite source for finding newspaper articles online.

➤ I know a lot of the sources, so I don't have to flail around. I also know how to formulate searches—select keywords, use features that help narrow the material down, follow trails, and mix it up by using a variety of approaches.

➤ I've become a lot more focused in how I search the Web now. I don't generally throw a lot of keywords at a search engine and let them fall where they may.

➤ Writing a book without email would take years longer!

➤ I definitely think writers should have their own Web sites. There's so much published, and so much noise, that you have to make a bit of your own noise to get the word out.

Appendix

Referenced Sites and Sources
www.infotoday.com/supersearchers

WEB SITES, SEARCH ENGINES, MAILING LISTS, NEWSGROUPS, ONLINE DATABASES, AND SOFTWARE

1. **411.com**
    www.411.com

2. **555-1212.com**
    www.555-1212.com

3. **About.com**
    www.about.com

4. **About.com's Urban Legends Page**
    www.urbanlegends.about.com

5. **About.com's Web Search**
    www.websearch.about.com

6. **Academy of American Poets**
    www.poets.org/index.cfm

7. **Access to Insight**
    www.accesstoinsight.org

8. **Ackerman's Costume Plates**
    www.costumes.org/pages/ackerman.htm

9. **Advanced Book Exchange**
    www.abebooks.com

10. **Advanced Imaging Magazine**
    www.advancedimagingmag.com

11. **Agent**
    www.forteinc.com/agent/tw.htm

12. **AHA! Poetry Site**
    Jane Reichold's AHA! Poetry Site

13. **Alexey Andreyev's Haiku Page**
    sharat.co.il/teneta/andreyev/haiku/html

14. **Alibris**
    www.alibris.com

15. **All-in-One Search Page**
    www.allonesearch.com

16. **AltaVista**
    www.altavista.com

17. **Amazing Bargains**
    www.amazingbargains.com

18. **Amazon.com**
    www.amazon.com

19. **American Cancer Society**
    www.cancer.org

20. **American Journalism Review**
    www.newslink.org

21. **American Society of Journalists and Authors (ASJA)**
    www.asja.org
    ASJA how-to-join page: www.asja.org/join01.php

22. **American Wind Energy Association**
    www.awea.org

23. **AnyWho**
    www.anywho.com

24. **AOL**
    www.aol.com

25. **Arachnophilia**
    www.arachnoid.com

26. **Arts & Letters Daily**
    www.cybereditions.com/aldaily/

27. **Ask Jeeves**
    www.askjeeves.com or www.ask.com

28. **AskSam SurfSaver**
    www.asksam.com

29. **Association for Cancer Online Resources**
    www.acor.org

30. **Association for Progressive Communicators**
    www.apc.org/

31. **Australian Slang**
    www.Koalanet.com.au/australian-slang.html

32. **Authors Guild**
    www.authorsguild.org

33. **Barnes & Noble**
    www.barnesandnoble.com

34. **Berinstein Research**
    www.berinsteinresearch.com

35. **Bibliofind**
    www.bibliofind.com

36. **Big Zoo**
    www.bigzoo.com

37. **BioMedNet**
    www.bmn.com

38. **Blue Ear Forum**
    www.blueear.com

39. **Bookfinders**
    www.hpbookfinders.co.uk

40. **BookMarket.com**
    www.bookmarket.com

41. **Books and Writers**
    www.booksandwriters.com

42. **Bookwire**
    www.bookwire.com

43. **Boston.com**
    www.boston.com

44. **Botanical.com**
    www.botanical.com

45. **Buddha-L**
    paml.net/groupsB/buddha-l.html

To subscribe, send email to listserv@LISTSERV.LOUISVILLE.EDU
In the body of the message, enter: subscribe buddha-l

46. **Buddhist Peace Fellowship**
    Email bpf@yahoogroups.com

47. **Budget Traveller's Guide to Sleeping in Airports**
    www3.sympatico.ca/donna.mcsherry/airports.htm

48. **Business Wire**
    www.businesswire.com/expertsource

49. **CancerBACUP**
    www.cancerbacup.org.uk

    Cancer Guide *see* **Steve Dunn's Cancer Guide**

50. **CARR-L (Computer Assisted Reporting & Research)**
    To subscribe, email listserv@ LISTSERV.louisville.edu
    Leave the subject line blank. In the body of the message enter: subscribe
    CARR-L

51. **Chicago Sun-Times**
    www.suntimes.com/index/

52. **Chicago Tribune**
    www.chicagotribune.com

53. **China News Digest**
    www.cnd.org

54. **Clariti**
    www.clariti.com

55. **Cliché Finder**
    www.westegg.com/cliche/

56. **ClicheSite.com**
    www.clichesite.com/index.asp

57. **CNET**
    www.cnet.com

58. **CNET News**
    www.news.com

59. **CNN**
    www.cnn.com

60. **Concierge.com**
    www.concierge.com

61. **Connected**
    www.connected.com

62. **Consumer World**
    www.consumerworld.org

63. **Contentious**
    www.contentious.com

64. **Contentville**
    www.contentville.com

65. **Copernic 2001**
    www.copernic.com

66. **Corbis Stock Market**
    www.corbisstockmarket.com

67. **Cordon Bleu**
    www.cordonbleu.net

68. **Cyndi's List**
    www.CyndisList.com

69. **Danny Sullivan's Search Engine Watch**
    www.searchenginewatch.com

70. **DejaNews**
    www.deja.com

71. **Delorme**
    www.delorme.com

72. **Dialog**
    www.dialog.com

73. **Direct-PR**
    www.direct-pr.com

74. **Discount Magazines**
    www.discountmagazines.com

75. **Ditto.com**
    www.ditto.com

76. **Dogpile**
    www.dogpile.com

77. **Dow Jones Interactive**
    www.djinteractive.com

78. **drkoop.com**
    www.drkoop.com

96. **Federal Communications Commission**
    www.fcc.gov/

97. **Find a Quotation**
    www.btinternet.com/~alexandergrant/quotes/finquoteframes.htm

98. **Find Articles**
    www.findarticles.com

99. **Findsame.com**
    www.findsame.com

100. **Florida Department of Corrections**
     www.dc.state.fl.us/index.html

101. **"Freudian Send"** article on Salon.com
     www.salon.com/21st/feature/1998/06/19feature.html

102. **Frommer's**
     www.frommers.com

103. **Go!zilla**
     www.gozilla.com

104. **Google**
     www.google.com

105. **Gopher**
     gopher://gopher.tc.umn.edu/

106. **Grateful Med**
     igm.nim.nih.gov

107. **Greg R. Notess's Search Engine Showdown**
     www.searchengineshowdown.com

108. **Guide to Literary Agents**
     literaryagents.org

109. *Ha'aretz* **Online**
     new.haaretz.co.il
     English edition: www3.haaretz.co.il/eng/htmls/1_1.htm

110. **Halfbakery**
     www.halfbakery.com

111. **Half.com**
     www.half.com

112. **Hal Higdon**
     www.halhigdon.com

113. **HeadlineSpot.com**
www.headlinespot.com

114. **Hollywood Reporter**
www.hollywoodreporter.com

115. **HotBot**
www.hotbot.com

116. **Hotel Discounts**
www.hoteldiscounts.com

117. **Hotmail**
www.hotmail.com

118. **Illinois Department of Corrections**
www.idoc.state.il.us/

119. **Infoplease Almanac**
www.infoplease.com

120. **Infoselect**
www.miclog.com

   Infotrieve *see* **Medline via Infotrieve**

121. **Institute for Global Communications**
www.igc.org

122. **InteliHealth**
www.intelihealth.com

123. **Internet Bookshop**
www.bookshop.co.uk

124. **Internet Movie Database**
www.imdb.com

125. **Internet Scout**
www.trentu.ca/library/internet/gennet.shtml

126. **Interpol Cultural Property Program**
www.usdoj.gov/usncb/cultprop/about/culturehome.htm

127. **Intranet Journal**
idm.internet.com

128. **IRE-L (Investigative Reporters and Editors)**
Email listproc@lists.missouri.edu
In the message body, enter: subscribe IRE-L your-name (insert your name)

129. **Itools**
www.itools.com/research-it/

130. **iVillage**
www.ivillage.com

131. **ixquick.com**
www.ixquick.om

132. **Jane Reichold's AHA! Poetry Site**
ahapoetry.com

Jim Romenesko's MediaNews
See **MediaNews (Jim Romenesko's)**

Jim Romenesko's Obscure Store and Reading Room
See **Obscure Store and Reading Room** (Jim Romenesko's)

133. **Jindagi's Wordsmith Page**
www.jindagi.com/wordsmith

134. **Joe deRouen's The Reference Desk**
www.sparkynet.com/jderouen/refdesk.html

135. **Journalism Section of the WWW Virtual Library**
www.trainer.com/vlj.html

136. **JOURNET-L (Discussion List for Journalism Education)**
Email listserv@listserv.american.edu
In the message body, enter: subscribe journet-l

137. **Journey Woman**
www.journeywoman.com

138. **Kirsch Foundation**
www.kirschfoundation.org/

139. *KMWorld*
www.kmworld.com

140. **Knopf Publishing**
www.randomhouse.com/knopf/poetry

141. **LaughNet (vomit jokes)**
www.laughnet.net/archive/crude/rbp_vomi.htm

142. **Leiden University**
www.leidenuniv.nl/ub/biv/specials.htm

143. **LexisNexis**
www.lexisnexis.com

144. **Library of Congress**
www.lcweb.loc.gov/

145. **Library of Congress catalog site**
catalog.loc.gov

146. *LinkUp*
www.infotoday.com/lu/lunew.htm

147. **List of Lists**
www.catalog.com/vivian/interest-group-search.html

148. **Liszt**
www.liszt.com

149. **Lockergnome**
www.lockergnome.com

150. *Los Angeles Times*
www.latimes.com

151. **Lung Cancer Online**
www.lungcanceronline.org

152. **Lycos**
www.lycos.com

153. **Mail-list.com**
www.mail-list.com

154. **Mapblast**
www.mapblast.com

155. **MapQuest**
www.mapquest.com

156. **Maps On Us**
www.mapsonus.com

157. **Martindale's The Reference Desk**
www-sci.lib.uci.edu/HSG/Ref.html

158. **MayoClinic.com**
www.mayoclinic.com

159. **Media Central**
www.mediacentral.com

160. **MediaNews (Jim Romenesko's)**
www.poynter.org/medianews

161. **Medline via Infotrieve**
www3.infotrieve.com
See also Medscape

162. **Medscape**
www.medscape.com

163. **Merck Manual Home Edition**
www.merck.com

164. **Merriam-Webster Online**
www.m-w.com

165. **Michael Moore**
www.michaelmoore.com

166. **Microsoft**
www.microsoft.com

167. **Money, Meaning & Choices Institute**
www.mmcinstitute.com

168. **Moreover**
www.moreover.com

169. **National Association for Poetry Therapy**
www.poetrytherapy.org

170. **National Cancer Institute**
www.cancernet.gov

171. **National Clearinghouse of Plastic Surgery Statistics**
www.plasticsurgery.org/mediactr/stats.htm

172. **National Institutes of Health**
www.nih.gov

173. **National Science Foundation**
www.nsf.gov

174. **Net-happenings**
listserv.classroom.com/archives/net-happenings.html

175. **NewsGuy**
www.newsguy.com

176. **NewsPage**
www.individual.com

177. **Newswise**
www.newswise.com

178. **New York Public Library Reference Desk**
www.nypl.org

179. *New York Times*
www.nytimes.com

180. *New York Times* **Book Site**
     www.nytimes.com/books

181. *New York Times* **List of Links**
     www.nytimes.com/library/tech/reference/cynavi.html

182. *New York Times* **Travel Section**
     www.nytimes.com/travel

183. **Nexis**
     www.nexis.com

184. **Nolo Press**
     www.nolo.com

185. **Northern Light**
     www.northernlight.com

186. **NUA Internet Surveys**
     www.nua.ie/surveys

187. **Obscure Store and Reading Room (Jim Romenesko's)**
     www.obscurestore.com

188. **Oncolink**
     www.oncolink.com

189. **Onelook**
     www.onelook.com

190. *Onion*
     www.theonion.com

191. **Online Book Initiative**
     ftp.std.com/obi/

192. **Online Dictionary Net**
     www.online-dictionary.net/

193. **Oprah.com**
     www.oprah.com

194. **Owsley Stanley**
     www.thebear.org/

195. **Padraic Cassidy's Web Page**
     home.earthlink.net/~cassidyny/jourlinks.htm

196. **Paris Hotels by Metro Stop**
     www.paris.org/Hotels/Metro

197. **PayPal**
     www.paypal.com

198. **PCWorld.com News**
     www.pcworld.com/news/index.asp

199. **Photonica**
     www.photonica.com

200. **Poetry and the Enneagram**
     www.breakoutofthebox.com/table6.htm

201. **Powell's Books**
     www.powells.com

202. **ProfNet**
     www.profnet.com

203. **ProFusion**
     www.profusion.com

204. **Project Gutenberg**
     www.promo.net/pg

205. **Publisher's Lunch**
     www.publisherslunch.com

206. *Publishers Weekly*
     www.publishersweekly.com

207. **Publist**
     www.publist.com

208. **Qpass**
     www.qpass.com

209. **Quack Watch**
     www.quackwatch.com

210. **Quikbook**
     www.quikbook.com

211. **Quoteland.com**
     www.quoteland.com

212. **Rageboy**
     www.rageboy.com

213. **Random House Author Links**
     www.randomhouse.com/author/links.html

214. **Random House Modern Library**
     www.randomhouse.com/modernlibrary

215. **Random House Resources**
     www.randomhouse.com/resources

216. **Rectal Foreign Bodies**
www.well.com/user/cynsa/newbutt.html

217. **Reference Desk**
www.refdesk.com
See also **Joe deRouen's The Reference Desk** and **Martindale's The Reference Desk**

218. **Regency Costume**
heyerlist.org/ghcost1.htm

219. **Research Central**
word.to/rc.html or www.levity.com/interbeing/rc.html

220. **Research Central Updates**
word.to/updates.html or www.levity.com/interbeing/updates.html

221. **Reuters**
www.reuters.com

222. **Rich Remsberg**
www.remsbergphoto.com

223. **Ridley Pearson**
www.ridleypearson.com

224. **Roller Coaster FAQ**
www.faqs.org/faqs/roller-coaster-faq

225. **Romance Writers' List (RW-L)**
To subscribe, send email to listserv@MAELSTROM.ST.JOHNS.EDU
In the body of the message, enter: subscribe rw-l

Romenesko, Jim *see* **MediaNews, Obscure Store and Reading Room**

226. **Salem, Oregon Online**
www.oregonlink.com

Salon.com *see* **"Freudian Send" article** on Salon.com

227. *Science* **magazine**
www.scienceonline.org

228. **Scientific American**
www.sciam.com

Search Engine Showdown *see* **Greg R. Notess's Search Engine Showdown**

229. **Search Engine Watch**
www.searchenginewatch.com

230. **Search IQ**
www.zdnet.com/searchiq/

231. **Shiki Internet Haiku Salon**
cc.matsuyama-u.ac.jp/~shiki/

232. **Sinusitis Support Newsgroup**
alt.support.sinusitis

233. *Slate*
www.slate.com

234. **SourceNet**
www.mediamap.com

235. **Space News**
space.com/spacenews

236. **SPJ-L (Society for Professional Journalists List)**
To subscribe, send email to listserv@LISTS.PSU.EDU
In the body of the message, enter subscribe spj-1

237. **Spot.com**
www.spot.com

"Stalking Law" *see* **United States Department of Justice "Stalking Law"**

238. **Steve Dunn's Cancer Guide**
www.cancerguide.org

239. **StrongWomen**
www.strongwomen.com

240. **Style.com**
www.style.com

241. *Syllabus* **magazine**
www.syllabus.com

242. **Symbols.com**
www.symbols.com

243. **Tasty Bits from the Technology Front**
tbtf.com

244. **Tellme**
www.tellme.com

245. *Literary Times*
www.tlt.com

246. *New Republic*
www.thenewrepublic.com

247. **The WELL**
www.well.com

248. **Thrive Online Health and Medical Section**
thriveonline.oxygen.com/health/

249. *Time* magazine
www.time.com/time

250. **Topica**
www.topica.com

251. **Tourism Offices Worldwide Directory**
www.towd.com

252. **Travelite FAQ**
www.travelite.org

253. **Union of Concerned Scientists**
www.ucsusa.org

254. **United States Census Bureau**
www.census.gov

255. **United States Department of Energy. Energy Information Administration**
www.eia.doe.gov

256. **United States Department of Justice "Stalking Law"**
www.ojp.usdoj.gov/vawo/grants/stalk98/chapter2.htm

257. **University of California at Berkeley** Internet Tutorial
www.lib.berkeley.edu/TeachingLib/Guides/Internet/FindInfo.html

Urban legends *see* **About.com's Urban Legends Page**

258. *USA Today*
www.usatoday.com

259. **Usenet**
groups.google.com

260. **Usenet Archive**
groups.google.com/googlegroups/archive_announce.html

261. **Vermont Eugenics: A Documentary History**
www.uvm.edu/~eugenics

262. **Vivisimo**
www.vivisimo.com

263. *Wall Street Journal* **"Personal Technology" column**
ptech.wsj.com

264. *Washington Post*
www.washingtonpost.com

265. *Washington Post* **Travel Section**
www.washingtonpost.com/wp-dyn/travel

266. **Washington State Government**
access.wa.gov

267. **WebMD**
www.webmd.com

268. **Web Pages That Suck**
www.webpagesthatsuck.com

WELL *see* **The WELL**

269. **WhatWeb!?**
word.to/whatweb.html or www.levity.com/interbeing/whatweb.html

270. **Wired News**
www.wired.com/news

Wordsmith Page *see* **Jindagi's Wordsmith Page**

271. **WorldCast**
www.fairlogic.com/worldcast/

272. **Worldwatch Institute**
www.worldwatch.org

273. **WriterL mailing list**
For fees and signup information, *see*
users.deltacomm.com/writerl/writerl/wlhome.htm

274. *Writer's Digest*
www.writersdigest.com

275. **WWW Virtual Library**
www.vlib.org

276. **WWW Virtual Library Hyper-Index of Buddhist Studies Resources**
www.uncwil.edu/iabs/vl

277. **Yahoo!**
www.yahoo.com

278. **Yahoo! Groups**
groups.yahoo.com

279. **Yahoo! Maps**
maps.yahoo.com

280. **Yahoo! Start Page**
my.yahoo.com

281. **Your Dictionary**
www.yourdictionary.com

282. **Zagat**
www.zagat.com

283. **ZDNet News**
www.zdnet.com/zdnn

ZDNet's Search IQ *see* **Search IQ**

BOOKS

284. *Competitor Intelligence: How to Get It, How to Use It,* by Leonard M. Fuld. John Wiley & Sons, 1985; out of print. (New edition: *The New Competitor Intelligence: The Complete Resource for Finding, Analyzing, and Using Information about Your Competitors.* Wiley, 1994.)

285. *Finding Images Online*, by Paula Berinstein. Pemberton Press, 1996. Distributed by Information Today, Inc. www.infotoday.com/catalog/books.htm

286. *Finding Statistics Online,* by Paula Berinstein. Information Today, Inc., 1998. www.infotoday.com/catalog/books.htm

287. *The WELL: A Story of Love, Death & Real Life in the Seminal Online Community*, by Katie Hafner. Carroll & Graf, 2001.

About the Author

For author Loraine Page, the writing of this book was a perfect marriage (if there is such a thing!) of her love of reading and her knowledge of the Internet. Since childhood, Loraine has been a voracious reader of fiction and nonfiction; since the mid-eighties, she has served as editor of *Link-Up,* a print publication that focuses on all the wonderful things that are available online. She started with *Link-Up* before anyone knew about the Internet and before you could get connected at lightning speed.

Loraine works from her home office on the East End of Long Island, New York. She is surrounded by heartachingly gorgeous vistas of sea, farmland, and orchards. And she's not too far from the incredible mansions of the Hamptons. It has been a lifelong ambition of hers to live in that region—and in the two and a half years she's been a resident, Long Island hasn't let her down.

From her office, spruced up with new lighting fixtures, sturdy shelving, and a meticulous paint job by supportive boyfriend Ed Herman, Loraine enjoys working on many editing and writing jobs. She takes special delight in announcing the arrival of a new book called *Mamma, Si Mangia? A Florentine Son Shares His Feisty Mother's Recipes* (Bright Sky Press, Spring 2002). This is an amusing narrative cookbook she co-wrote with her neighbor; his talented wife supplied the hilarious drawings.

Writing and editing are only half the story. Loraine is a serious amateur photographer who exhibits and wins awards for her color photography, an endeavor she's been passionate about for eleven years. Lately her focus has been seascapes and landscapes. She's inspired almost every time she takes a drive on the lovely island she calls home.

About the Editor

Reva Basch, executive editor of the Super Searcher book series, has written four books of her own: *Researching Online For Dummies* (Hungry Minds, 2nd edition with Mary Ellen Bates), *Secrets of the Super Net Searchers* (Information Today, 1996), *Secrets of the Super Searchers* (Information Today, 1993), and *Electronic Information Delivery: Evaluating Quality and Value* (Gower, 1995). She has edited and contributed chapters, introductions, and interviews to several books about the Internet and online information retrieval. She was the subject of a profile in *WIRED* magazine, which called her "the ultimate intelligent agent."

Prior to starting her own business in 1986, Reva was Vice President and Director of Research at Information on Demand, a pioneering independent research company. She has designed front-end search software for major online services; written and consulted on technical, marketing, and training issues for both online services and database producers; and published extensively in information industry journals. She has keynoted at international conferences in Australia, Scandinavia, and the United Kingdom, as well as North America.

Reva is a Past-President (1991–1992) of the Association of Independent Information Professionals and a member of the Special Libraries Association. She has a degree in English literature, *summa cum laude*, from the University of Pennsylvania, and a master's degree in Library Science from the University of California, Berkeley. She began her career as a corporate librarian, ran her own independent research business for ten years, and has been online since the mid-1970s.

Reva lives on the remote northern California coast with her husband, cats, and satellite access to the Internet.

Index

More Great Books from Information Today, Inc.

Electronic Styles
A Handbook for Citing Electronic Information

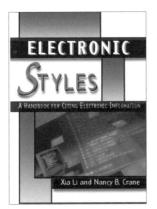

By Xia Li and Nancy Crane

The second edition of the best-selling guide to referencing electronic information and citing the complete range of electronic formats includes text-based information, electronic journals and discussion lists, Web sites, CD-ROM and multimedia products, and commercial online documents.

1996/214 pp/softbound/ISBN 1-57387-027-7 $19.99

The Wordwatcher's Guide to Good Grammar & Word Usage
Authoritative Answers to Today's Grammar and Usage Questions

By Morton S. Freeman
Foreword by Edwin Newman

From former nationally syndicated "Word Watcher" columnist Morton S. Freeman comes *The Wordwatcher's Guide to Good Grammar & Word Usage*. Arranged alphabetically by keyword in question-and-answer format to facilitate quick and easy reference, the book offers expert advice on grammar and usage problems that face both the professional and amateur writer every day.

Medford Press/Plexus/1998/296 pp/softbound/ ISBN 0-9666748-0-4 $19.95

Super Searchers in the News
The Online Secrets of
Journalists and News Researchers

By Paula J. Hane • Edited by Reva Basch

Professional news researchers are a breed apart. The behind-the-scenes heroes of network newsrooms and daily newspapers, they work under intense deadline pressure to meet the insatiable, ever-changing research needs of reporters, editors, and journalists. Here, for the first time, 10 news researchers reveal their strategies for using the Internet and online services to get the scoop, check the facts, and nail the story. If you want to become a more effective online searcher and do fast, accurate research on a wide range of moving-target topics, don't miss *Super Searchers in the News*.

Supported by the Super Searchers Web page.

2000/256 pp/softbound/ISBN 0-910965-45-5 $24.95

Super Searchers Go to the Source
The Interviewing and Hands-On Information
Strategies of Top Primary Researchers—
Online, on the Phone, and in Person

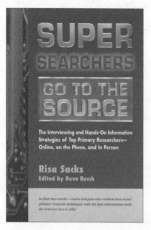

By Risa Sacks • Edited by Reva Basch

For the most focused, current, in-depth information on any subject, nothing beats going directly to the source—to the experts. This is "Primary Research," and it's the focus of the seventh title in the "Super Searchers" series. From the boardrooms of America's top corporations, to the halls of academia, to the pressroom of the *New York Times*, Risa Sacks interviews 12 of the best primary researchers in the business. These research pros reveal their strategies for integrating online and "off-line" resources, identifying experts, and getting past gatekeepers to obtain information that exists only in someone's head.

Supported by the Super Searchers Web page.

2001/420 pp/softbound/ISBN 0-910965-53-6 $24.95

The Extreme Searcher's Guide to Web Search Engines

A Handbook for the Serious Searcher, 2nd Edition

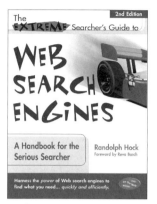

By Randolph Hock
Foreword by Reva Basch

In this completely revised and expanded version of his award-winning book, the "extreme searcher," Randolph (Ran) Hock, digs even deeper, covering all the most popular Web search tools, plus a half-dozen of the newest and most exciting search engines to come down the pike. This is a practical, user-friendly guide supported by a regularly updated Web site.

2001/250 pp/softbound/ISBN 0-910965-47-1 $24.95

"Ran Hock is the Mario Andretti of Web Searching."

—Chris Sherman, co-author, *The Invisible Web*

Editorial Peer Review

Its Strengths and Weaknesses

By Ann C. Weller

This important book is the first to provide an in-depth analysis of the peer review process in scholarly publishing. Author Weller (Associate Professor and Deputy Director at the Library of the Health Sciences, University of Illinois at Chicago) offers a carefully researched, systematic review of published studies of editorial peer review in the following broad categories: general studies of rejection rates, studies of editors, studies of authors, and studies of reviewers. The book concludes with an examination of new models of editorial peer review intended to enhance the scientific communication process as it moves from a print to an electronic environment. *Editorial Peer Review* is an essential monograph for editors, reviewers, publishers, professionals from learned societies, writers, scholars, and librarians who purchase and disseminate scholarly material.

2001/360 pp/hardbound/ISBN 1-57387-100-1 $44.50

The Invisible Web
Uncovering Information Sources
Search Engines Can't See

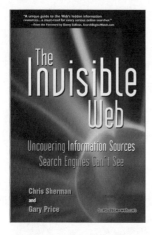

By Chris Sherman and Gary Price

Most of the authoritative information accessible over the Internet is invisible to search engines. This "Invisible Web" is largely comprised of content-rich databases from universities, libraries, associations, businesses, and government agencies. Authors Chris Sherman and Gary Price introduce you to top sites and sources and offer tips, techniques, and analysis that will let you pull needles out of haystacks every time. Supported by a dedicated Web site.

2001/450 pp/softbound/ISBN 0-910965-51-X
$29.95

The Modem Reference
The Complete Guide to PC Communications, 4th Edition

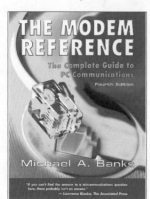

By Michael A. Banks

Now in its fourth edition, this popular handbook explains the concepts behind computer data, data encoding, and transmission, providing practical advice for PC users who want to get the most from their online operations. In his uniquely readable style, author and techno-guru Mike Banks (*The Internet Unplugged*) takes readers on a tour of PC data communications technology, explaining how modems, fax machines, computer networks, and the Internet work. He provides an in-depth look at how data is communicated between computers all around the world, demystifying the terminology, hardware, and software. *The Modem Reference* is a must-read for students, professional online users, and all computer users who want to maximize their PC fax and data communications capabilities.

2000/306 pp/softbound/ISBN 0-910965-36-6 $29.95